American Nightmare

T0358750

TRANSGRESSIONS: CULTURAL STUDIES AND EDUCATION

Cultural studies provides an analytical toolbox for both making sense of educational practice and extending the insights of educational professionals into their labors. In this context *Transgressions: Cultural Studies and Education* provides a collection of books in the domain that specify this assertion. Crafted for an audience of teachers, teacher educators, scholars and students of cultural studies and others interested in cultural studies and pedagogy, the series documents both the possibilities of and the controversies surrounding the intersection of cultural studies and education. The editors and the authors of this series do not assume that the interaction of cultural studies and education devalues other types of knowledge and analytical forms. Rather the intersection of these knowledge disciplines offers a rejuvenating, optimistic, and positive perspective on education and educational institutions. Some might describe its contribution as democratic, emancipatory, and transformative. The editors and authors maintain that cultural studies helps free educators from sterile, monolithic analyses that have for too long undermined efforts to think of educational practices by providing other words, new languages, and fresh metaphors. Operating in an interdisciplinary cosmos, *Transgressions: Cultural Studies and Education* is dedicated to exploring the ways cultural studies enhances the study and practice of education. With this in mind the series focuses in a non-exclusive way on popular culture as well as other dimensions of cultural studies including social theory, social justice and positionality, cultural dimensions of technological innovation, new media and media literacy, new forms of oppression emerging in an electronic hyperreality, and postcolonial global concerns. With these concerns in mind cultural studies scholars often argue that the realm of popular culture is the most powerful educational force in contemporary culture. Indeed, in the twenty-first century this pedagogical dynamic is sweeping through the entire world. Educators, they believe, must understand these emerging realities in order to gain an important voice in the pedagogical conversation.

Without an understanding of cultural pedagogy's (education that takes place outside of formal schooling) role in the shaping of individual identity – youth identity in particular – the role educators play in the lives of their students will continue to fade. Why do so many of our students feel that life is incomprehensible and devoid of meaning? What does it mean, teachers wonder, when young people are unable to describe their moods, their affective affiliation to the society around them. Meanings provided young people by mainstream institutions often do little to help them deal with their affective complexity, their difficulty negotiating the rift between meaning and affect. School knowledge and educational expectations seem as anachronistic as a ditto machine, not that learning ways of rational thought and making sense of the world are unimportant.

But school knowledge and educational expectations often have little to offer students about making sense of the way they feel, the way their affective lives are shaped. In no way do we argue that analysis of the production of youth in an electronic mediated world demands some "touchy-feely" educational superficiality. What is needed in this context is a rigorous analysis of the interrelationship between pedagogy, popular culture, meaning making, and youth subjectivity. In an era marked by youth depression, violence, and suicide such insights become extremely important, even life saving. Pessimism about the future is the common sense of many contemporary youth with its concomitant feeling that no one can make a difference.

If affective production can be shaped to reflect these perspectives, then it can be reshaped to lay the groundwork for optimism, passionate commitment, and transformative educational and political activity. In these ways cultural studies adds a dimension to the work of education unfilled by any other sub-discipline. This is what *Transgressions: Cultural Studies and Education* seeks to produce – literature on these issues that makes a difference. It seeks to publish studies that help those who work with young people, those individuals involved in the disciplines that study children and youth, and young people themselves improve their lives in these bizarre times.

American Nightmare

Donald Trump, Media Spectacle, and Authoritarian Populism

Douglas Kellner
UCLA Graduate School of Education and Information Studies,
Los Angeles, USA

SENSE PUBLISHERS
ROTTERDAM/BOSTON/TAIPEI

A C.I.P. record for this book is available from the Library of Congress.

ISBN: 978-94-6300-786-3 (paperback)
ISBN: 978-94-6300-787-0 (hardback)
ISBN: 978-94-6300-788-7 (e-book)

Published by: Sense Publishers,
P.O. Box 21858,
3001 AW Rotterdam,
The Netherlands
https://www.sensepublishers.com/

Cover image © Roymieco A. Carter

Printed on acid-free paper

TABLE OF CONTENTS

INTRODUCTION

Explaining the Donald Trump phenomenon is a challenge that will occupy critical theorists of U.S. politics for years to come. My first take on the Trump phenomenon is that Donald Trump won the Republican primary contest and is now a contender in the U.S. Presidential Election because he is the *master of media spectacle*, a concept that I've been developing and applying to U.S. politics and media since the mid-1990s.[1] In this study, I will first discuss Trump's use of media spectacle in his business career, in his effort to become a celebrity and reality-TV superstar, and his political campaign. Then I shall examine how Trump embodies Authoritarian Populism and has used racism, nationalism, xenophobia, Islamophobia, and the disturbing underside of American politics to mobilize his supporters in his successful Republican primary campaign and in the hotly contested 2016 general election.

The Trump phenomenon is a *teachable moment* that helps us understand the changes and contour of U.S. politics in the contemporary moment and the role of broadcast media, new media and social networking, and the politics of the spectacle. Trump reveals the threat of authoritarian populism, a phenomenon that is now global in scope, and the dangers of the rise to power of an individual who is highly destructive, who represents the worst of the 1 percent billionaire business class. Trump masquerades as a "voice of the forgotten man," as he advances a political agenda that largely benefits the rich and the military, and is a clear and present danger to U.S. democracy and global peace, constituting an American Nightmare for the world. Trump's rise to global celebrity and now political power is bound up with his use of media spectacle so, I begin my study with analysis of Trump and the politics of the spectacle.

DONALD TRUMP AND THE POLITICS
OF THE SPECTACLE

I first came up with the concept of media spectacle to describe the key
phenomenon of US media and politics in the mid-1990s. This was the
era of the O.J. Simpson murder case and trial, the Clinton sex scandals,
and the rise of cable news networks like Fox, CNN, and media MSNBC
and the 24/7 news cycle that has dominated US politics and media
since then.[2] The 1990s was also the period when the Internet and
New Media took off so that anyone could be a political commentator,
player, and participant in the spectacle, a phenomenon that accelerated
as New Media morphed into Social Media and teenagers, celebrities,
politicians, and others wanting to become part of the networked virtual
world joined in.

The scope of the spectacle has thus increased in the past decades with
the proliferation of new media and social networking like Facebook,
YouTube, Twitter, Instagram, Skype, and the like that increases the
breadth and participation of the spectacle. By "media spectacles" I am
referring to media constructs that present events which disrupt ordinary
and habitual flows of information, and which become popular stories
which capture the attention of the media and the public, and circulate
through broadcasting networks, the Internet, social networking, smart
phones, and other new media and communication technologies. In a
global networked society, media spectacles proliferate instantaneously,
become virtual and viral, and in some cases becomes tools of socio-
political transformation, while other media spectacles become mere
moments of media hype and tabloidized sensationalism.

Dramatic news and events are presented as media spectacles and
dominate certain news cycles. Stories like the 9/11 terror attacks,
mass shooting, Hurricane Katrina, Barack Obama and the 2008 U.S.
presidential election, and in 2011 the Arab Uprisings, the Libyan
revolution, the UK Riots, the Occupy movements and other major
media spectacles of the era, cascaded through broadcasting, print, and
digital media, seizing people's attention and emotions, and generating

complex and multiple effects that may make 2011 as memorable a year in the history of social upheaval as 1968.[3]

In today's highly competitive media environment, *"Breaking News!"* of various sorts play out as media spectacle, including mega-events like wars, other spectacular terrorist attacks, extreme weather disasters, or, political insurrections and upheavals. These spectacles assume a narrative form and become focuses of attention during a specific temporal and historical period, that may only last a few days, but may come to dominate news and information for extended periods of time. Examples include the O.J. Simpson Trial and the Clinton sex/impeachment scandal in the mid-1990s, the stolen election of 2000 in the Bush/Gore presidential campaign, and natural and other disasters that have significant destructive effects and political implications, such as Hurricane Katrina, the BP Deepwater Horizon Oil Spill, or the Fukushima-Daiichi nuclear catastrophe. Media spectacles can even become signature events of an entire epoch as were, arguably, the 9/11 terrorist attacks which inaugurated a historical period that I describe as Terror War (Kellner, 2003).

I've argued since 2008 that the key to Barack Obama's success in two presidential elections is because he became a master of media spectacle, blending politics and performance in carefully orchestrated media spectacles (Kellner, 2009, 2012). Previously, the model of the mastery of presidential spectacle was Ronald Reagan who everyday performed his presidency in a well-scripted and orchestrated daily spectacle. Reagan was trained as an actor and every night Ron and Nancy reportedly practiced his lines for the next day performance like they had done in their Hollywood days. Reagan breezed through the day scripted with a teleprompter and well-orchestrated media events, smiling frequently, and pausing to sound-bite the line of the day.

Now in the 2016 election, obviously Donald Trump has emerged as a major form of media spectacle and has long been a celebrity and master of the spectacle with promotion of his buildings and casinos from the 1980s to the present, his reality-TV shows, self-aggrandizing events, and now his presidential campaign. Hence, Trump is empowered and enabled to run for the presidency in part because media spectacle has become a major force in US politics, helping to determine elections, government, and, more broadly, the ethos and nature of our culture and political sphere, and Trump is a successful creator and manipulator of the spectacle.

I would also argue that in recent years U.S. wars have been orchestrated as media spectacle, recalling Bush Jr's 2003 Iraq shock and awe campaign for one example. Likewise, terrorism has been orchestrated as media spectacle since the 9/11 attack that was the most spectacular and deadly attack on the US heartland in history. As we know too well, school and mass shootings which can be seen as a form of domestic terrorism, have become media spectacles with one taking place in 2015 in Virginia on live TV, while the stock market, weather, and every other form of life can become part of a media spectacle. Hence, it is no surprise that political campaigns are being run as media spectacles and that Knights of the Spectacle like Donald Trump are playing the spectacle to win the presidency, although it is far from certain that the Donald will become King of the Spectacle.

Trump's biographies reveal that he was driven by a need to compete and win,[4] and entering the highly competitive real estate business in New York in the 1980s, Trump saw the need to use the media and publicity to promote his celebrity and image. It was a time of tabloid culture and media-driven celebrity and Trump even adopted a pseudonym "John Baron" to give the media gossip items that touted Trump's successes in businesses, with women, and as a rising man about town.[5]

Trump derives his language and behavior from a highly competitive and ruthless New York business culture combined with an appreciation of the importance of media and celebrity to succeed in a media-centric hypercapitalism. Hence, to discover the nature of Trump's "temperament," personality, and use of language, we should recall his reality-TV show *The Apprentice* which popularized him into a supercelebrity and made the Donald a major public figure for a national audience. Indeed, Trump is the first reality-TV candidate who runs his campaign like a reality-TV series, boasting during the most chaotic episodes in his campaign that his rallies are the most entertaining, and sending outrageous Tweets into the Twitter-sphere which than dominate the news cycle on the ever-proliferating mainstream media and social networking sites. Hence, Trump is the first celebrity candidate whose use of the media and celebrity star power is his most potent weapon in his improbable and highly surreal campaign.[6]

THE APPRENTICE, TWITTER, AND
THE SUMMER OF TRUMP

Since Trump's national celebrity derived in part from his role in the reality-TV series *The Apprentice*,[7] we need to interrogate this popular TV phenomenon to help explain the Trump phenomenon. The opening theme music "For the Love of Money", a 1973 R&B song by The O'Jays, established the capitalist ethos of the competition for the winning contestant to get a job with the Trump organization, and obviously money is the key to Trump's business and celebrity success, although there is much controversy over how rich Trump is, and, so far, he has not released his tax returns to quell rumors that he isn't as rich as he claims, that he does not contribute as much to charity as he has stated, and that many years he pays little or no taxes.

In the original format to *The Apprentice*, several contestants formed teams to carry out a task dictated by Trump, and each "contest" resulted with a winner and Trump barking "you're fired" to the loser. Ironically, some commentators believe that in the 2012 presidential election Barack Obama beat Mitt Romney handily because he early on characterized Romney as a billionaire who liked to fire people, which is ironic since this is Trump's signature personality trait in his business, reality-TV, and now political career, which has seen him fire two campaign managers and more advisors by August 2016.

The Apprentice premiered in January 2004, and after six seasons, a new format was introduced: *The Celebrity Apprentice*. The celebrity apprentice series generally followed the same premise as the original, but with celebrities as contestants participating to win money for their chosen charities, rather than winning a job opportunity with the Trump organization. There have been seven seasons of *The Celebrity Apprentice* since 2008, although NBC announced on June 29, 2015 that it was severing all business ties with Trump due to the latter's comments about Mexican immigrants, but has said its relationship with the producer of the series Mark Burnett and the show will continue.

When NBC started negotiating with Trump concerning the reality TV-series in 2002, according to NBC producer Jeff Gaspin, the network was not sure that the New York-centric real estate mogul would have a national resonance and the initial concept envisaged different billionaires each season hiring an apprentice. The show immediately got good ratings and Trump became a popular TV figure as he brought the contestants into his board room in Trump Tower, appraised their performances, insulted and sometimes humiliated those who did not do well, and fired the loser.[8]

The Apprentice's TV Producer Mark Burnett broke into national consciousness with his hit reality-TV show *The Survivor*, which premiered in 1992 a neo-Darwinian epic of alliances, backstabbing, and nastiness. The series provides an allegory of how one succeeds in the dog-eat-dog business world in which Donald Trump has thrived, and spectacularly failed as many of the books about him document. Both Burnett and Trump share the same neo-Darwinian (a)social ethos of 19th century ultracompetitive capitalism with some of Donald Trump's famous witticisms proclaiming:

- When somebody challenges you unfairly, fight back—be brutal, be tough—don't take it. It is always important to WIN!
- I think everyone's a threat to me.
- Everyone that's hit me so far has gone down. They've gone down big league.
- I want my generals kicking ass.
- I would bomb the shit out of them.
- You bomb the hell out of the oil. Don't worry about the cities. The cities are terrible.[9]

In any case, *The Apprentice* made Trump a national celebrity who became well-known enough to run for president and throughout the campaign Trump has used his celebrity to gain media time. Further, *The Apprentice* provided a Trumpian pedagogy of how to succeed in the cut-throat corporate capitalist business world with the show illustrating what aggressive, highly competitive, and sometimes amoral tactics are needed to win and gain success, and provided for a generation the message that winning was everything and that losing was devastating.[10]

In addition to his campaign's ability to manipulate broadcast media, Trump is also a heavy user of Twitter and tweets obsessively throughout the day and night. Indeed, Trump may be the first major Twitter candidate, and certainly he is the one using it most aggressively and frequently. Twitter was launched in 2006, but I don't recall it being used in a major way in the 2008 election, although Obama used Facebook and his campaign bragged that he had over a million "Friends" and used Facebook as part of his daily campaign apparatus.

Twitter is a perfect vehicle for Trump as you can use its 140 character framework for attack, bragging, and getting out simple messages or posts that engage receivers who feel they are in the know and involved in TrumpWorld when they receive his tweets. When asked at an August 26, 2015, Iowa event as to why he uses Twitter so much, he replied that it was easy, it only took a couple of seconds, and that he could attack his media critics when he "wasn't treated fairly." Trump has also used Instagram – an online mobile photo-sharing, video-sharing and social networking services that enables its users to take pictures and short videos, and share them on a variety of social networking platforms, such as Facebook, Twitter, Tumblr and Flickr.

Twitter is perfect for General Trump who can blast out his opinions and order his followers what to think. It enables Businessman and Politician Trump to define his brand and mobilize those who wish to consume or support it. Trump Twitter gratifies the need of Narcissist Trump to be noticed and recognized as a Master of Communication who can bind his warriors into an on-line community. Twitter enables the Pundit-in-Chief to opine, rant, attack, and proclaim on all and sundry subjects, and to subject TrumpWorld to the indoctrination of their Fearless Leader.

Hence, Trump is mastering new media as well as dominating television and old media through his orchestration of media events as spectacles and daily Twitter Feed. In Trump's presidential campaign kickoff speech on June 16, 2015, when he announced he was running for President, Trump and his wife Melania dramatically ascended down the escalator at Trump Towers, and the Donald strode up to a gaggle of microphones and dominated media attention with his drama. The opening speech of his campaign made a typically inflammatory remark that held in thrall news cycles for days when he stated: "The U.S. has become a dumping ground for everybody else's problems. [Applause] Thank you. It's true, and these are the best and the finest. When Mexico sends its people, they're not sending their best. They're not sending you. They're not sending you. They're sending people that have lots of problems, and they're bringing those problems with us. They're bringing drugs. They're bringing crime. They're rapists. And some, I assume, are good people."

This comment ignited a firestorm of controversy and provided a preview of Things to Come concerning vile racism, xenophobia, Islamophobia, and the other hallmarks of Trump's Cacophony of Hate. Debate over Trump's assault on undocumented immigrants would come to dominate daily news cycles of the Republican primaries and would continue to play out in the general election in Fall 2016. In the lead up to the first Republican primary debate in Fall 2015, Donald Trump got the majority of media time, and his daily campaign appearances and the Republican primary debates became media spectacles dominated by Trump. Every day that Trump had a campaign event, the cable news networks would hype the event with crawlers on the bottom of the TV screen proclaiming "Waiting for Trump," with air-time on cable TV dominated by speculation on what he would talk about. Trump's speeches were usually broadcast live, often in their entirety, a boon of free TV time that no candidate of either party was awarded. After the Trump event, for the rest of the day the pundits would dissect what he had said and his standing vis-à-vis the other Republican candidates. If Trump had no campaign event planned, he would fire off a round of Tweets against his opponents on his highly active Twitter account – which then would be featured on network cable news discussions as well as social media.

Hence, Trump's orchestration of media spectacle and a compliant mainstream media was a crucial factor in thrusting Trump ever further into the front runner status in the Republican primaries and winning for him the overwhelming amount of media attention and eventually the Republican nomination. The first major quantitative study released notes that from mid-June 2015 after Trump announced he was running through mid-July, Trump was in 46% of the news media coverage of the Republican field, based on Google news hits; he also got 60% of Google news searches, and I will bet that later academic studies will show how he dominated all media from newspapers to television to Twitter and new media to social networking during the Republican primaries and then during the general election.[11]

At a press conference on August 26, 2015, before his appearance at a rally in Dubuque Iowa, Trump bragged how all three US cable news networks, as well as the other big three networks and even foreign news networks, were following him around all day, broadcasting all his live campaign appearances, and even his appearance for Jury duty in New York one day (he didn't have to serve and cable news anchors led off that night with ordinary people who had been waiting all day to see if they would be enrolled to serve on a jury who were asked what Trump had been doing all day, if he'd said anything, and so on, clearly a waste of news space and sign that Trump was dominating Republican primary coverage).

The August 26, 2015 Iowa event was the day that a Univision anchor Jorge Ramos tried to interrupt Trump's press conference to challenge Trump on immigration, in which Trump had his operatives throw Ramos out, but then let him back in to create another media spectacle of Trump vs Ramos as they battled it out debating immigration, letting Trump dominate yet another news cycle.

The same day, Trump bragged about how one major media insider told him that it was the "Summer of Trump" and that it was amazing how he was completely dominating news coverage. Trump also explained, correctly I think, why he was getting all the media attention: "RATINGS," he explained, "it's ratings, the people love me, they want to see me, so they watch TV when I'm on." And I do think it is ratings that leads the profit-oriented television networks to almost exclusively follow Trump's events and give him live TV control of the audience. In his 1989 book, *Fast Capitalism*, and *Speeding Up Fast Capitalism*, a sequel to his earlier book, Ben Agger presented a framework for analyzing mutations in society, culture, and politics that have made possible a Donald Trump.[12] Without a media-saturated "fast capitalism" and media-centric politics, new technologies like Twitter and social networking, and a celebrity culture that has morphed into politics, there could never be a Donald Trump. Trump's ability to dominate the mediascape of contemporary capitalism and now sectors of the political scene is facilitated by quasi-religious beliefs that the allegedly successful businessman (who may or may not be a billionaire) has the qualifications to lead, and there is no doubt but that his celebrity status attracts devoted followers.

TRUMP, CAPITALISM, AND
THE ART OF BRANDING

Trump rose to prominence in New York during the Reaganite '80s as an embodiment of wild, entrepreneurial cowboy capitalism in an era of deregulation, the celebration of wealth, and the "greed is good" ethos of Wall Street, enabled by the Reagan administration. Trump's success was tied to an unrestrained finance capital that loaned him immense sums of money, often with minimal and problematic collateral, to carry through his construction projects. Trump was an extravagant consumer with a three story penthouse at the top of Trump Towers, a 118 room mansion in Palm Beach, Florida Mar-A-Lago that he immediately opened for TV interview segments, and an obscene array of properties. He flaunted a yacht bought from Saudi arms dealer Adnan Khashoggi, and a personal airplane to jet set him around the world to luxury resorts. Trump was featured on TV shows like *Life Styles of the Rich and Famous,* and his life-style was the subject of multi-page spreads in fashion and other popular magazines, making Trump the poster-boy for excessive "conspicuous consumption," of a degree that I doubt Veblen could have imagined.[13]

Trump's book *The Art of the Deal* (1987) provides a revealing portrait of the unrestrained capitalism of the go-go '80s, as well insight into the psyche and behavior of Donald Trump, hypercapitalist.[14] The book celebrates "dealing" and "the art of the deal" illustrated by Trump moving from the family real estate business of Queens and Brooklyn onto the Magic Isle of Manhattan where the Donald moved in his mid-20s to become a celebrated real estate whiz kid. He tells in detail how he transformed the shabby and faded Commodore Hotel, across from Grand Central Station, into the Grand Hyatt, which he saw as part of the "Reviving [of] 42nd Street" (pp. 119ff). The centerpiece of the celebration of Deal Artist Donald is the story of the building of "Trump Tower: The Tiffany Location" (pp. 145ff.), which stands as Trump's most striking construction deal. Trump recounts his moving to Atlantic Casino and beginning to take over and build casinos (195ff), his "Battle for Hilton" with mogul Steve Wynn (225ff), his short time in the United States Football League (USFL), where he ended up with an unsuccessful suit against the NFL and saw the collapse of the USFL and loss of his team (273ff). A highpoint for Trump is his rebuilding of the Wollman Ice Rink, finishing a project under-time and under-budget that the city was not able to do, providing for Trump a lesson on the superiority of free enterprise construction opposed to bungling government projects.

Indeed, Trump's book and his life-endeavor serves as an ideological exemplar of free-market capitalism, with government providing obstruction, obstacles to overcome, and sometimes bureaucratic morass that blocks completely the Donald's projects which he presents as noble and invigorating for a sometimes faltering economy. Of course, sometimes government can aide construction project and Trump brags about how his father Fred controlled Brooklyn politicos to get his projects done. Donald himself tells of how negotiations with New York city and state officials helped him get tax abatements, contracts, and permits to build his pet projects. Indeed, an important part of the trajectory of Trump's business life is manipulating government to aid him in his projects and he continues to brag on the campaign trail how he bought and used politicians.

Trump's financial fortunes hit the economic slowdown that followed the Reagan orgy of unrestrained capitalism in the late 1980s,[15] and in the 1990s Trump almost became bankrupt. Fittingly, Trump had overinvested in the very epitome of consumer capitalism, buying a string of luxury gambling casinos in Atlantic City. The financial slump hit Trump's overextended casinos, driving him to put them on the market. The banks called in loans on his overextended real estate investments, and he was forced to sell off properties, his yacht, and other luxury items. Having temporarily lost his ability to borrow from finance capital to expand his real estate business, Trump was forced to go into partnerships in business ventures, and then sold the Trump name that was attached to an array of consumer items ranging from water to vodka, and men's clothes to fragrances.

Trump's two books *Trump: Surviving at the Top* (1990) and *Trump: The Art of the Comeback* (1997) provide an incisive portrait of the

14

beginning of Trump's business troubles in the late '80s and early '90s (*Surviving*) and then his collapse into near bankruptcy and partial comeback later in the decade (*Art of the Comeback*).[16] *Surviving at the Top* tells of the business struggles and setbacks of the era, his very public unravelling of his celebrated marriage to Ivana that was a tabloid sensation for months, punctuated by what he sees as his great triumphs of the era, including beating TV-personality Merv Griffin out for Atlantic City resort deals (91ff), the purchase of the fabled Plaza Hotel (pp. 110ff), his purchase of the East Coast Trump Shuttle (pp. 132ff), his purchase of one of the world's most grandiose and expensive yachts (pp. 150ff), his adventures with gambling casinos (pp. 163ff), and his celebrity friendships with Boxer Mike Tyson and others (pp. 191ff). Indeed, two of his books feature a "Week in the Life" chapter where the Donald notes all the famous people from all walks of business, political, and celebrity life that he talks to and meets every day. All of his books drop names and ooze out gossip and his personal likes and hates concerning the rich and famous, or those who cross his path and help him (thumbs up!), or hinder him (thumbs down!).

Trump: The Art of the Comeback (1997) presents the drama of the collapse of many of Trump's businesses in the early 1990s and his restructuring of his loans with bankers which he presents as a "comeback." Before the title page, there are TRUMP'S TOP TEN COMEBACK TIPS which include banalities like "Stay Focused," "Be Passionate," and "Go With Your Gut" punctuated with dubious advice like "Play Golf" and "Be Lucky," sprinkled with "tips" expressing Trump's pessimistic neo-Darwinian world-view that I discussed above and which informs his presidential campaign like "Be Paranoid," "Go Against the Tide," and "Get Even" – perhaps the guiding principle of Trump's life.

It is clear from his books that Trump grossly overextended himself, and invested in many dubious projects, such as his three Atlantic City casinos which went bankrupt, or he was forced to sell. *Comeback* drips with venom against those bankers who refused to help Trump and pressured him to pay off his loans, as well as others with whom he had conflicts during the decade. Trump attacks his tormentors in short vignettes that present his enemies in vitriolic and insulting terms, and then he flings a heap of insults upon them, as he would later do with his political opponents. His nastiness and vindictiveness is shocking in the book which raises serious questions about his temperament. For example, he unloads on super lawyer Bert Fields, fires him (Bert said he quit), and concludes: "I think he's highly overrated, and his high legal fees were a continuing source of irritation to me. I continued to use the firm but not Fields" (p. 103). Or, note his attacks on the press and authors who have written books critical of him:

> The media is simply a business of distortion and lies… the press writes distorted and untruthful things about me almost daily. For example, books written by Harry Hurt and Jack O'Donnell, a disgruntled former employee I hardly even knew, were so of the mark that twenty-five or fifty years from now, if people use this crap as a backlog on me, it will be very unfair. These guys didn't know me, didn't like me, and only wanted to produce a really negative product. Stories they told about my life and business were seldom correct, nor did these authors want them to be. The good news is that nobody bought their garbage, and I was able to blunt the impact of the books' sales by publicly explaining the facts. This is why neither book was successful—I really knocked the shit out of both of them and took down their credibility. (pp. 185–186)

In fact, both of these books by Hurt and O'Donnell are well-written and documented, and note that Trump does not mention any particulars that either author got wrong. To say that "[s]tories they told about my life and business were seldom correct" is ludicrous, and both books continue to sell and illuminate aspects of Trump's life and times.

In *Comeback*, Trump's misogyny is blatantly apparent he attacks his wife Ivana, exposing painful details of their divorce and legal battles (pp. 118ff). Trump took over the Miss Universe Contest and attacks the then current Miss Universe for gaining fifty pound and being an embarrassment to him, "sitting there plumply" (p. 106). In a chapter "The Women in (and out) of My Life," Trump brags about all the women who come on to him (his second marriage is breaking up during the period, so he is a player again), and goes on ad nauseam about "Katarina Witt, the great Olympic figure-skating champion and how she allegedly pursued him, and then when he didn't respond leaked to tabloids that she had "spurned" the Donald (pp. 126ff). He discusses a civic activist Madeleine Palaise who opposed one of his construction projects in particularly negative terms and generally puts on display excessively retrograde attitudes toward women.

Yet the most revealing chapter concerning his deeply-rooted sexism is encapsulated in the "tip" to "Always Have a Prenuptial Agreement" and spelled out in the chapter "The Art of the Prenup: The Engagement Wring" (pp. 143ff). Trump is fanatic on the importance of businessmen to get a lawyer to write a prenuptial contract before marriage. In the unnumbered "Tips" page at the opening of his book Trump writes: "Anyone in a complicated business should be institutionalized if he or she gets married without one. I know firsthand that you can't come back if you're spending all of your time fighting for your financial life with a spouse." Trump sees marriage as a predatory battle of the sexes and women as predators who use their sexuality and charms to get the better of men, warning that women are the most "powerful" sex and "far stronger than men" (121), who should beware of any women who shows interest in a relationship or marriage, surely a retrograde and paranoid view of women.

Whereas *The Art of the Deal* describes impressive achievements giving the Donald bragging rights, his following two books try to white wash his failures and decline as a major real estate constructor (the family business). As noted above, Trump was forced from the '90s into the 21st century to find partnerships for his enterprises, since banks were reluctant to loan him money for his projects because he had so overextended himself and failed in so many ventures. Hence, Trump was forced to sell his name to an array of products to keep his cash flow going, or find partners to put up the money in any business ventures.

Indeed, Trump has been particularly assiduous in branding the Trump name and selling himself as a businessman, a celebrity, and now as a presidential candidate. No doubt, Trump's books are largely an exercise in branding the company name and rebranding it when it becomes tarnished. In fact, Trump's presidential campaign represents an obscene branding of a hypercapitalist pig into a political candidate whose campaign is run on bombast, dominating on a daily basis the mediascape, and gaining the attention of voters/consumers (with the willing complicity of the cable news networks and with the help of his Twitter feed). Obviously, Trump is orchestrating political theater in his presidential run, his theatrics are sometimes entertaining, and, as I noted earlier, his candidacy represents another step in the merger between entertainment, celebrity and politics (in which Ronald Reagan played a key role as, our first actor President). Yet Trump is the first major candidate to pursue politics as entertainment and thus to collapse the distinction between entertainment, news, and politics. He is also the first authoritarian populist to have been a party nominee for President in recent times.

DONALD TRUMP AND AUTHORITARIAN POPULISM

Much has been made of Donald Trump's character and whether he is fit to be president of the United States. In the following analysis, I want to suggest that the theories of Erich Fromm and his fellow German-Jewish refugees known as the "Frankfurt School" provide an analysis of authoritarian populism that helps explicate Trump's character, his appeal to his followers, and in general the Trump phenomenon.[17]

Erich Fromm was a German Jewish intellectual and psychoanalyst who was affiliated with the Frankfurt School, a group of German Jews and progressives who left Hitler's Germany in the early 1930s and settled in the United States, developing critical theories of fascism, contemporary capitalism, and Soviet Marxism from a theoretical standpoint that combines Marx, Freud, Weber, Nietzsche and other radical theorists and critics of Western civilization.[18] Fromm was the group's Freud expert who was affiliated with the Frankfurt Psychoanalytic Institute in Germany, and was a practicing analyst in Germany and then the United States. After breaking with the Frankfurt school in the late-1930s, Fromm went on to becoming a best-selling author and radical social critic in the United States.

Fromm was a strong critic of Hitler and German fascism and I believe that his major books and some key ideas help explain the character, presidential campaign, and supporters of Donald Trump. Hence, in this discussion, I develop a Frommian analysis of Trump and his followers and take on the issue of how American authoritarian populism would look. This project begins with Fromm's *Escape from Freedom*, which explains how in modernity individuals submitted to oppressive and irrational regimes and in particular how Germans submitted to Hitler and fascism.[19] *Escape* combines historical, economic, political, ideological and socio-psychological analysis, as is typical of the best multidimensional work of Fromm and the Frankfurt School, and provides a model that we can apply to analyzing Trump and our current political situation.

Certainly, Trump is not Hitler and his followers are not technically fascists,[20] although I believe that we can use the terms *authoritarian populism* or *neo-fascism* to explain Trump and his supporters.[21] Authoritarian movements ranging from German and Italian fascism to Franco's Spain to Latin American and other dictatorships throughout the world center on an authoritarian leader and followers who submit to their leadership and demands. I will argue that Donald Trump is an authoritarian leader who has mobilized an authoritarian populist movement that follows his leadership. Arguably, Trump is an authoritarian populist in the traditions of Ronald Reagan and Margaret Thatcher. Like Reagan, Trump comes out of the entertainment industry and was a popular celebrity as he announced his candidacy in summer 2015 thanks in part to his television celebrity as every mainstream media outlet touted his announcing his candidacy. Trump does not share the conservative ideology of Reagan and Thatcher, although he shares their electoral strategy of taking a populist pose claiming to represent the people against the political establishment.

Yet Trump lacks Reagan's disciplined skills as a performer and Thatcher's "Iron Lady" self-discipline and political acumen. Instead, Trump shoots from the lip and cannot resist insults, attacks, impolitic language and rants against those who dare to criticize him. While Trump does not have a party apparatus or ideology like the Nazis, parallels to Nazism appeared clear to me last summer at Trump's August 21, 2015, Alabama mega-rally in Mobile, Alabama. I watched all afternoon as the cable news networks broadcast nothing but Trump, hyping up his visit to a stadium where he was expecting 30–40,000 spectators, the biggest rally of the season. Although only 20-some thousand showed up, which was still a "huge" event in the heat of summer before the primaries had even begun in earnest, Trump's flight into Alabama on his own Trump Jet and his rapturous reception by his admirers became the main story of the news cycle, as did many such daily events in what the media called "the summer of Trump."

What I focused on in watching the TV footage of the event was how the networks began showing repeated images of Trump flying his airplane over and around the stadium before landing and then cut away to big images of the Trump Jet every few minutes. This media spectacle reminded me of one of the most powerful propaganda films of all time – Leni Riefenstahl's *Triumph of the Will* – a German Nazi propaganda film of 1935. *Triumph* focuses on Hitler flying in an airplane through the clouds, looking out the window at the crowds below, landing, and driving through mass crowds applauding him as his proceeded through the streets of Nuremburg for a mass rally. The crowds along the way and in the stadium greeted Hitler with rapture as he entered the spectacle of a highly touted and orchestrated Nuremburg mass Nazi rally that Riefenstahl captured on film.

I do not know if the Trump operatives planned this parallel, or if it was just a coincidence, but it is clear that Trump, like Hitler, has organized a fervent mass movement outside of the conventional political party apparatuses. The anger and rage that Fromm attributed to Nazi masses in *Escape From Freedom* is also exhibited in Trump's followers as is the *idolatry* toward their Fuhrer, who arguably see Trump as the *magic helper* who will solve their problems by building a giant wall to keep out the threatening Other, a Fairy Tale scenario that Fromm would have loved to deconstruct.[22]

Like followers of European fascism in the 1930s, Trump's supporters over the years have suffered economic deprivation, political alienation, humiliation, and a variety of hard times, and they appear to be looking for a political savior to help them out with their problems and to address their grievances. Trump proposes magical solutions like a wall along the Mexican border that will keep out swarms of immigrants that he claims are taking away jobs in the U.S., as well as committing waves of crime. Trump claims he will create millions of "great" jobs without giving specific plans – a claim refuted by his problematic business record that includes many bankruptcies, hiring of foreign workers to toil on his projects, some of whom he does not pay, and failures to pay many subcontractors who worked on his projects.[23]

Trump thus presents himself as a Superhero who will magically restore the U.S. to greatness, provide jobs and create incredible wealth, and restore the U.S. to its rightful place as the world's Superpower. In this Fairy Tale, the billionaire King will fight and destroy all the Nation's domestic and foreign enemies and the Superman will triumph and provide a Happy Ending for the U.S. people.[24]

While Trump plays the role of the *Ubermensch* (Superman or Higher Man) celebrated by the Nazis and embodies their *Fuhrerprincip* (leadership principle), Trump is a very American form of the Superhero, and lacks the party apparatus, advanced military forces, and disciplined cadres that the Nazis used to seize and hold power. Like other rightwing American populists, Trump bashes the Federal Reserve, the U.S. monetary system, Wall Street hedge fund billionaires, and neoliberal globalization, in the same fashion as Hitler attacked German monopoly capitalism. While Hitler ranted against monopoly capitalists, at the same time he accepted big donations from German industrialists, as brilliantly illustrated in the famous graphic by John Heartfield "the meaning of the Hitler salute" which showed Hitler with his hand up in the Nazi salute, getting bags of money from German capitalists.[25] Just as Hitler denounced allegedly corrupt and weak party politicians in the Weimar Republic, Trump decries all politicians as "idiots," "stupid," or "weak" – some of the would-be strongman's favorite words. In fact, Trump even attacks lobbyists, and claims he alone is above being corrupted by money, since he is self-financing his own campaign (which is not really true but seems to impress his followers).[26]

Trump has his roots in an American form of populism that harkens back to figures like Andrew Jackson, Huey Long, George Wallace, Pat Buchanan and, of course, the American carnival barker and snake oil salesman.[27] Like these classical American demagogues, Trump plays on the fears, grievances, and anger of people who feel that they have been left behind by the elites. Like his authoritarian populist predecessors, Trump also scapegoats targets from Wall Street to a feared mass of immigrants allegedly crossing the Mexican border and pouring into the States, overwhelming and outnumbering a declining White population.[28]

Trump's followers share antecedents in the Know Nothing movement of the 1850s, the Ku Klux Klan movement which achieved popularity and media in the 1920s, with Donald's father Fred Trump arrested at one of its rallies,[29] and the movement that made George Wallace a popular candidate in the 1960s. Alabama Governor George Wallace stirred up racist resentment in his 1968 campaign, as with Trump, there was violence at his rallies, and he appealed to largely white and alienated and resentful voters. Further, Trump and his followers exemplify Richard Hofstader's analysis of *The Paranoid Style in American Politics* which traces lineages between racist, xenophobic, and paranoid tendencies in 19th century rightwing populists and Joseph McCarthy and his followers.[30]

More recently, Trump's rightwing populist roots and supporters draw on the Tea Party movement which emerged in 2010 as a revolt against establishment politics. Like Trump's supporters, advocates of the Tea Party were a rightwing populist movement that loathed Obama, were anti-government, anti-immigrant, and pro-police, military, and hardright law and order.[31] Some of their candidates were elected to Congress and other positions and some of the movement supported Donald Trump, whereas others supported Ted Cruz and even took a NeverTrump position. Hence, the Tea Party is better seen as an anticipation of Trump's movement than a key component of it.

Like the alienated and angry followers of authoritarian populist movements throughout the world, Trump's admirers had suffered under the vicissitudes of capitalism, globalization, and technological revolution. For decades, they have watched their jobs being moved overseas, displaced by technological innovation, or lost through unequal economic development amid increasing divisions between rich and poor. With the global economic crisis of 2007–08, many people lost jobs, housings, savings, and suffered through a slow recovery under the Obama administration. The fact that Obama was the first black president further outraged many who had their racism and prejudices inflamed by eight years of attacks on Obama and the Obama administration by rightwing media and the Republican Party.

Indeed, Donald Trump was one of the most assiduous promotor's of the "birther" myth, erroneously claiming that Barack Obama was born in Africa and was thus not eligible to serve as President of the United States.[32] In the 2008 presidential election, Trump made a big show of insisting that Obama display his birth certificate to prove he was born in the U.S., and although the Obama campaign provided photocopies of the original birth certificate in Hawaii and notices of his birth in Honolulu newspapers at the time, Trump kept insisting they were frauds and many of his followers continue to believe the myth that Obama was not born in the USA.[33]

Yet unlike classic dictators who are highly disciplined with a fixed ideology and party apparatus, Trump is chaotic and undisciplined, viciously attacking whoever dares criticize him in his daily Twitter feed or speeches, thus dominating the daily news cycles with his outrageous attacks on Mexicans, Muslims, and immigrants, or politicians of both parties who dare to criticize him. Trump effectively used the broadcast media and social media to play the powerful demagogue who preys on his followers' rage, alienation, and fears. Indeed, by March 2016, media companies estimated that Trump received far more media coverage than his Republican Party contenders, and by June *MarketWatch* estimated that he had received $3 billion worth of free media coverage.[34] Yet, at his whim, Trump bans news media from his rallies, including *The Washington Post*, if they publish criticisms that he does not like.

Like followers of European fascism, the Trump's authoritarian populist supporters are driven by rage: they are really angry at the political establishment and system, the media, and economic and other elites. They are eager to support an anti-establishment candidate who claims to be an outsider (which is only partly true as Trump has been a member of the capitalist real estate industry for decades, following his father, and has other businesses as well, many of which have failed).[35] Trump provokes his followers rage with classic authoritarian propaganda techniques like the Big Lie, when he falsely repeats over and over that immigrants are pouring across the border and committing crime, that all his primary opponents, the media, and Hillary Clinton are "big liars," and that he, Donald Trump is the only one telling the truth – clearly the biggest lie of all.[36]

Trump's anti-immigrant and racist rhetoric, his Islamophobia, and his xenophobic nationalism plays into a violent racist tradition in the U.S. and activates atavistic fears of other races and anger among his white followers. Like European fascism, Trump draws on restorative nostalgia and promises to "Make America Great Again" – a regressive return to an earlier never specified time. To mobilize his followers, Trump both appeals to nostalgia and manipulates racism and nationalism, while playing to the vile side of the American psyche and the long tradition of nationalism, America First-ism, and xenophobia, wanting to keep minorities and people of color outside of the country and "in their place."

Gun rights fanatics were one of Trump's strong core constituencies and never had a candidate (who previously had no visible connection to gun culture) so rabidly defended gun rights while attacking Clinton and Democrats who he falsely accused as dead-set on taking guns away from people.[37] Trump also played on the grievances and resentments of evangelicals who feared that in a secular culture their religious rights would be curtailed,[38] nationalists who believed the nation was in decline and resented as well as liberals who allegedly pushed civil rights agendas that favored people of color.

An article in *The New Yorker* by Evan Osmos describes Trump's followers as "The Fearful and the Frustrated" with the subtitle: "Donald Trump's nationalist coalition takes shape – for now."[39] The reporter has been following Trump's campaign and interviewing his followers and the article reveals that Trump has not only attracted Tea Party followers, but also white nationalists with journals like *The Daily Stormer* "who urged white men to 'vote for the first time in our lives for the one man who actually reps our interests.'" Osmos interviews all over the country other members of far right neo-Nazi, white supremacist, and ultra nationalist groups and concludes:

> From the pantheon of great demagogues, Trump has plucked some best practices – William Jennings Bryan's bombast, Huey Long's wit, Father Charles Coughlin's mastery of the airwaves – but historians are at pains to find the perfect analogue, because so much of Trump's recipe is specific to the present. Celebrities had little place in U.S. politics until the 1920 Presidential election, when Al Jolson and other stars from the fledgling film industry endorsed Warren Harding. Two decades ago, Americans were less focused on paid-for politicians, so Ross Perot, a self-funded billionaire candidate, did not derive the same benefit as Trump from the perception of independence."[40]

Like fascists and authoritarian populists, Trump thus presents himself as the Superhero leader who can step in from outside and solve the problems that Washington and politicians have created. In the form of *authoritarian idolatry* described by Fromm,[41] his followers appear to believe that Trump alone can stop the decline of the United States and make it "great" again. Over and over, Trump supporters claim that he is the only one who talks about issues like immigration, problems with Washington and politics, and the role of money in politics. Trump promotes himself as the tough guy who can stand up to the Russians and Chinese, and to "America's enemies." In the Republican primaries, he presented himself as "the most militarist" guy in the field and promised to build up the US military, and to utterly destroy ISIS and America's enemies, restoring the U.S. to its superpower status, which he says was lost by the Obama administration. Trump embodies the figure to excess of strong masculinity that Jackson Katz describes as a key motif in recent U.S. presidential elections.[42] With his bragging, chest-pounding, and hypermacho posturing, Trump provides a promise of restoration of White Male Power and authority that will restore America to its' greatness.

Macho Superman Trump will make "America Great Again" and vanquish all its enemies. Indeed, "Make America Great Again" is perhaps the defining motif of Trump's presidential campaign – a slogan he puts on his baseball caps that he hands out or sells to his supporters. The baseball hat makes it appear that Trump is an ordinary fellow, and links him to his followers as one of them, a clever self-presentation for an American authoritarian populist. Sporting a baseball cap on the campaign trail is especially ironic, given that Trump appears to have borrowed this fashion from award-winning, progressive documentary filmmaker Michael Moore who is perhaps the anti-Trump in the U.S. political imaginary. Further, in his speech at the Republican convention, this shouting red-faced, orange-haired demagogue presented himself as the "voice of the forgotten men and women" – a Depression era phrase of the Roosevelt administration which Trump inflects toward his white constituency who believes they have been forgotten and passed over in favor of the rich, minorities, and celebrities. In the speech and on the campaign trail, Trump uses the discourse of national crisis also deployed by classic fascist and authoritarian regimes to describe the situation in the U.S. and the need for a savior to solve all the problems. In contrast to the Nazis, however, Trump tells his followers that it's his deal-making skills as a supercapitalist billionaire which credentials him to be the President, and he induces his followers to believe he will make a "great deal" for them and "Make America Great Again."

The slogan "Make America Great Again" refers for some of Trump's supporters to a time where White Males ruled and women, people of color, and others knew their place. It was a time of militarism where U.S. military power was believed to position America as the ruler of the world—although as the ambiguous Cold War and U.S. military defeats in Vietnam and the uncontrollable spaces of Iraq and Afghanistan, this era of American greatness was largely a myth. Yet the slogan is vague enough that Trump's followers can create a fantasy of a "great" past and dream that Trump will resurrect it – a fantasy conceit nourished by many authoritarian leaders in the 20th century.

Trump is replicating this phenomenon of *authoritarian populism* and his campaign exhibits in many ways the submission to the leader and the cause found in classic authoritarian movements. Yet Trump is also the embodiment of trends toward celebrity politics and the implosion of politics and entertainment which is becoming an increasingly important feature of U.S. politics (see Note 6). Further, Trump is a master of PR and promoting his image, and would even call up journalists pretending to be a PR agent to get gossip items planted about him in newspapers (see Note 5). More disturbing is the oft-played footage of Trump mimicking a *New York Times* reporter with a disability.[43] Indeed, there is a sinister side to Trump as well as the cartoonish and creepy side.

Trump is thus an authoritarian populist and his campaign replicates in some ways the submission to the leader and the cause found in classic authoritarian movements. In some ways, however, it is Mussolini, rather than Hitler, who Trump most resembles. Hitler was deadly serious, restrained, and repressed, while Trump is comical, completely unrestrained, and arguably unhinged.[44] Curiously, on February 28, 2016, Trump used his Twitter feed to post a quote attributed to Mussolini, which compared the Italian dictator to Trump, and in an interview on NBC's "Meet the Press" that morning said: "It's a very good quote," apparently not bothered by being associated with Mussolini.[45] There were also news clips that showed Trump speaking, chin jutting out in Mussolini-like fashion, and making faces and performing gestures that seemed to mimic characteristics associated with Mussolini.[46]

Like Mussolini, Trump has a buffoonish side which his mobocracy finds entertaining, but which turns off more serious folks. Trump is the embodiment of trends toward celebrity politics and the implosion of politics and entertainment which is becoming an increasingly important feature of U.S. politics.[47] Further, there is a disturbing side to Trump, and in the next section I shall use the work of Erich Fromm to engage Trump's sinister aspects and personality type.

DONALD TRUMP AS AUTHORITARIAN POPULIST: A FROMMIAN ANALYSIS

In this section, I want to discuss in detail how Erich Fromm's categories can help describe Trump's character, or "temperament," a word used to characterize a major flaw in Trump in the 2016 U.S. presidential campaign. In *The Anatomy of Human Destructiveness* (1973), Fromm engages in a detailed analysis of the authoritarian character as sadistic, excessively narcissistic, malignantly aggressive, vengeably destructive, and necrophilaic, personality traits arguably applicable to Trump.[48] I will systematically inventory key Frommian socio-psychoanalytic categories and how they can be applied to Trump to illuminate his authoritarian populism.

Trump, in Freudian terms used by Fromm, can be seen as the *Id* of American politics, often driven by sheer aggression, narcissism, and, rage. If someone criticizes him, they can be sure of being attacked back, often brutally. And notoriously, Trump exhibits the most gigantic and unrestrained *Ego* yet seen in US politics constantly trumping his wealth,[49] his success in business, how smart he is, how women and all the people who work for him love him so much, and how his book *The Art of the Deal* is the greatest book ever written – although just after saying that to a Christian evangelical audience, he back-tracked and said *The Bible* is the greatest book, but that his *Art of the Deal* is the second greatest, which for Trump is the bible of how to get rich and maybe how to win elections.

Trump, however, like classical fascist leaders, has an underdeveloped *Superego*, in the Freudian sense that generally refers to a voice of social morality and conscience. While Trump has what we might call a highly developed Ego that has fully appropriated capitalist drives for success, money, power, ambition, and domination, biographies of Trump indicate that he has had few life-long friends, discards women with abandon (he is on his third marriage), and brags of his ruthlessness in destroying competitors and enemies.[50]

Drawing on Fromm's *Escape from Freedom* and other writings, and studies of *The Authoritarian Personality* done by the Frankfurt School,[51] Trump obviously fits the critical theory model of an *authoritarian character* and his 2016 Presidential campaign replicates in some ways the submission to the leader and the movement found in authoritarian populism. Further, Trump clearly exhibits traits of the *sadist* who Fromm described as "a person with an intense desire to control, hurt, humiliate, another person," a trait that is one of the defining feature of the authoritarian personality."[52]

Frommian sadism was exemplified in Trump's behavior toward other Republican Party candidates in primary debates, in his daily insults of all and sundry, and at Trump rallies in the behavior of him and his followers toward protestors. During the 2016 campaign cycle, a regular feature of a Trump rally involved Trump supporters yelling at, hitting, and even beating up protestors, while Trump shouts "get them out! Out!'" When one Trump follower sucker punched a young African American protestor in a campaign event at Fayetteville, N.C. on March 9, 2016, Trump offered to pay his legal expenses after he was arrested.

Despite the accelerating violence at Trump rallies during the summer of 2016, and intense pressure for Trump to renounce violence at his campaign events and reign in his rowdy followers, Trump deflected blame on protestors and continued to exhibit the joy of a sadist controlling his environment and inflicting pain on his enemies, as police and his followers continued to attack and pummel protestors at his events. When Trump's campaign manager Corey Lewandowski was charged with assault on a reporter, Trump continued to defend him, although Lewandowski was fired when the Trump campaign brought in veteran political hired gun Paul Manafort, who had served dicatators like Angolan terrorist Jonas Savimbi, the Pakistani Inter-Service Intelligence with notorious al Queda links, Ukrainian dictator and Putin ally Viktor Yanukovych, foreign dictators such as Ferdinand Marcos and Joseph Mobuto of Zaire, and many more of the Who's Who list of toxic dictators and world-class rogues (among whom one must number Manafort and Trump). Apparently, involved in a power struggle within the Trump campaign with Manafort, Lewandowski was fired.

Fromm's analysis of the *narcissistic personality* in *The Sane Society* (1955) and *The Anatomy of Human Destructiveness* also helps explain the Trump phenomenon, given that Trump is one of the most narcissistic figures to appear in recent U.S. politics.[53] For Fromm: "Narcissism is the essence of all severe psychic pathology. For the narcissistically involved person, there is only one reality, that of his own thought, processes, feeling and needs. The world outside is not experienced or perceived objectively, i.e., as existing in its own terms, conditions and needs."[54]

In a study of Hitler in *The Anatomy of Human Destructiveness*, Fromm develops further his analysis of the "extremely narcissistic person" and links extreme narcissism with the authoritarian leader in language that provides an uncanny anticipation of Donald Trump: "he is interested only in himself, his desires, his thoughts, his wishes; he talked endlessly about his ideas, his part, his plans; the world is interesting only as far as it is the object of his schemes and desires; other people matter only as far as they serve him or can be used; he always knows better than anyone else. This certainty in one's own ideas and schemes is a typical characteristic of intense narcissism."[55]

Michael D'Antonio is his book *Never Enough. Donald Trump and the Pursuit of Success* sees Trump as the exemplification of the "culture of narcissism" described by Christopher Lasch and notes:

> Trump was offered as a journalist's paragon of narcissism at least as far back as 1988. The academics and psychologists got involved a few years later would go on to make the diagnosis of Trump into a kind of professional sport. Trump makes an appearance in texts for the profession, including *Abnormal Behavior in the 21st Century* and *Personality Disorders and Older Adults: Diagnosis, Assessment, and Treatment.* He also appears in books for laypeople such as The *Narcissism Epidemic: Loving in the Age of Entitlement*; *Help! I'm in Love with a Narcissist;* and *When you Love a Man Who Loves himself.*[56]

31

Trump's extreme narcissism is evident in his obsession with putting his name on his buildings or construction sites, ranging from Trump Towers to (now failed) casinos in New Jersey to golf courses throughout the world. Yet Trump often fails, as in his attempt in 1979 to get a New York convention center named after his father, or his failure to get a football stadium named the Trumpdome, in an unsuccessful endeavor in the mid-1980s, when Trump, first, was blocked from getting an NFL football team, and then saw the USFL football league in which he had a team collapse.[57] Indeed, Democratic Party opposition research, as well as all voters and especially Trump supporters, should read the Trump biographies to discover the grubby details of all of Trump's failed projects, including a string of casinos in New Jersey and at least four major bankruptcies in businesses that he ran into the ground, since Trump grounds his claims for the presidency on the alleged success of his business ventures.[58]

Further, Trump embodies as well what Fromm identifies as the *nonproductive character orientation*, in particular the *exploitative*, which characterizes Trump's activity as a hypercapitalist billionaire, and the *marketing orientation*, which defines his business activity and self-promotion, his self-aggrandizement on his television shows like *The Apprentice*, and his recent presidential campaign. Trump embodies the orientation of "having over being" that was a central distinction of Fromm's later work, and arguably Trump combines the sadism of the authoritarian character type with out-of-control narcissism and a man who cannot possess enough wealth and power.[59]

Although Trump presents himself as the People's Choice and voice of the Forgotten Man, Trump himself has been especially exploitative of his workers, and in his life style and habitus lives in a radically different world than the hoi polloi. For example, in 1985, Trump bought a 118 room mansion in Palm Beach, Florida Mar-A-Lago that he immediately opened for TV interview segments and "that launched Donald's second career as a frequent start of 'Lifestyles of the Rich and Famous.'"[60] Trump became an exemplar of what Veblen described as "conspicuous consumption,"[61] a trait he continues to cultivate to excess up to the present. Indeed, Trump has been particularly assiduous in branding the Trump name and selling himself as a celebrity and now as a presidential candidate his entire adult life.

These personality traits, however, arguably attract Trump's followers who envy his billionaire status, his marketing and entertainment dimensions, and his lavish display of wealth, as well as to take pleasure in his attacks on immigrants, Muslims, other politicians, and the political establishment in general. This potent combination of envy and anger motivate identification with Trump by his supporters, even though there is really no rational basis to believe that this arrogant asshole of the Super Rich will champion their interests, or maybe they think with Trump they'll win the lottery, strike it rich, and roll the dice that Trump will enable them to fulfill their dreams and restore their ego and pride. Indeed, it could be that we are seeing the end of rational choice politics as Trump followers pursue their aggressive instincts with the hope of a self-proclaimed billionaire savior, rather than pursuing their economic and class interests.[62]

However, perhaps the conceptual key to Trump's authoritarian personality is related to Fromm's analysis of *"malignant aggression"* developed in *The Anatomy of Human Destructiveness* (1973). Trump arguably embodies both spontaneous and "bound in character structure" aspects of what Fromm characterizes as malignant aggression (270ff), spontaneously lashing out at anyone who dares to criticize him, and arguably his deep-rooted extremely aggressive tendencies help characterize Trump and connect him to classic authoritarian leaders. Trump typically describes his opponents as "losers" and uses extremely hostile language in attacking all of his opponents and critics. In his TV reality show *The Apprentice* (2005–2015), which features a group of competitors battling for a high-level management job in one of Trump's organizations, each segment ended with Trump triumphantly telling one of the contestants that "you're fired!" – a telling phrase that Trump filed for a trademark in 2004, and which revealed his sadistic joy in controlling and destroying individuals.

As Henry Giroux argues, "loser" for Trump "has little to do with them losing in the more general sense of the term. On the contrary, in a culture that trades in cruelty and divorces politics from matters of ethics and social responsibility, 'loser' is now elevated to a pejorative insult that humiliates and justifies not only symbolic violence, but also (as Trump has made clear in many of his rallies) real acts of violence waged against his critics, such as members of the Movement for Black Lives."[63] "Loser" means exclusion, humiliation, and abjection, a trope prevalent in sports, business, and politics where "winners take all" and losers are condemned to the ignominy of failure, the ultimate degradation in Trump's amoral capitalist universe.

Hence, I would argue that both Trump's TV reality show *The Apprentice* and Trump's behavior on the show and in public embody Frommian analysis of malignant aggression. Indeed, it has not been enough for Trump to defeat his Republican Party opponents in the 2016 Presidential election, but he must destroy them. He described his initial major opponent Jeb Bush as "low energy" and gloated as Jeb failed to gain support in the primaries and dropped out of the race early. Rubio is dismissed as "little Marco," Cruz is disparaged as "Lyin' Ted," and as for the hapless Ben Carson, Trump tweeted: "With Ben Carson wanting to hit his mother on head with a hammer, stab a friend and [claiming that Egyptian] Pyramids [were] built for grain storage – don't people get it?" Curiously, despite these malignant insults, the ineffable Carson endorsed Trump after he dropped out of the race, and continues to support him on TV.[64]

Already during the primary campaign, Trump began referring to Hillary Clinton as "Crooked Hillary," and by the time of the Republican National Convention his audiences shouted out "lock her up" whenever Trump uses the phrase. In a Pavolovian gesture, Trump has his troops orchestrated to perform in rituals of aggression, as, for instance, when he refers to the wall he promises to build on the Mexican border, and calls to his audience, "who's gonna pay," the audience shouts out in a booming unison: "Mexico!"

In my memory, there has never been such insulting and disparaging rhetoric used against one's opponents in modern elections, although such labelling and invective seemed to work for Trump in the Republican primaries, pointing to a vulgarization of the public sphere that would have appalled Erich Fromm. Trump's favorite words include positives like "incredible," "amazing," "huge," "fabulous," and "really great." Above all, he loves "winners" and mocks "losers," while using negatives like "idiots," "stupid," "cowards," and "weak," one of his favorite terms for his political opponents or pundits who criticize him. He defines his opponents in negative terms, repeating endlessly that Jeb Bush lacks energy, implying he's weak and not manly, while in the *Fox News* debate when Rand Paul interrupted him, Nasty Donald fired back that Paul had not been hearing him correctly, and chided him for his weak debate performance that night (I read later that Paul uses a hearing aid, so this snide comment revealed the bullying side of Trump and that if you stand up to him, you will almost surely be bullied, which so far has been the case).

In fact, Trump's attitudes and behavior toward women exhibit traits of Fromm's malignant aggression, as well as blatant sexism. The day after the initial Republican debate on August 6, 2015, Trump complained about *Fox News* debate moderator Megyn Kelly, whining: "She gets out and she starts asking me all sorts of ridiculous questions. You could see there was blood coming out of her eyes, blood coming out of her wherever."[65]

As outrage over Trump's comment spread, he took to Twitter to deny that he meant to imply Kelly was menstruating, claiming in a Tweet: "Mr. Trump made Megyn Kelly look really bad – she was a mess with her anger and totally caught off guard. Mr. Trump said "blood was coming out of her eyes and whatever" meaning nose, but wanted to move on to more important topics. Only a deviant would think anything else."[66]

Trump's appalling reference to Megyn Kelly's blood is paralleled by his off-color comments about Hillary Clinton ranting that her use of the bathroom during a Democratic Party debate was "too disgusting" to talk about – "disgusting, really disgusting," he repeated. He also delighted in recounting how Ms. Clinton got "schlonged" by Barack Obama when she lost to him in the 2008 Democratic primary.

For weeks following, Trump continued war with "crazy Megyn" leading *Fox News* to respond in her defense:

> Donald Trump's vitriolic attacks against Megyn Kelly and
> his extreme, sick obsession with her is beneath the dignity
> of a presidential candidate who wants to occupy the highest

office in the land. Megyn is an exemplary journalist and one of the leading anchors in America – we're extremely proud of her phenomenal work and continue to fully support her throughout every day of Trump's endless barrage of crude and sexist verbal assaults. As the mother of three young children, with a successful law career and the second highest rated show in cable news, it's especially deplorable for her to be repeatedly abused just for doing her job."[67]

Later in his campaign, Dumbass Donald attacked MSNBC hosts Mika Brzezinski and Joe Scarborough for bad-mouthing him and threatened to "tell the real story" about them, which presumably had to do with their sexual relation. Trump assured his followers: "If people hit me, I will certainly hit back," he said. "That will never change."

Trump's aggressive and compulsive Tweets and daily insults against his opponent exemplify the *"vengeful destructiveness"* described by Fromm as part of malignant aggression, which is another defining trait of the authoritarian leader. As an example of Trump's propensities toward vengeful destructiveness, take Trump's remarks toward Judge Gonzalo Curiel's Mexican heritage who Trump claimed had an "Absolute Conflict" in being unable to rule impartially in a fraud lawsuit against Donald Trump's now defunct real estate school, Trump University, because he was Mexican-American. Trump claimed that the Mexican-American heritage of the judge, who was born in Indiana to Mexican immigrants, was relevant because of Trump's campaign stance against illegal immigration and his pledge to seal the southern U.S. border with Mexico. Despite the fact that the Judge was ruling on a case involving Trump University, the Donald just couldn't help making nasty vengeful and destructive remarks against the Judge, who was a highly respected Jurist and who was widely defended by the legal community against Trump's attack.

Further, Trump threatened the Republican Party in March 2016 with riots at its summer convention if there was any attempt to block his nomination, and in August 2016 as his poll numbers Fell, and Hillary Clinton widened her lead, Trump claimed that the election is "rigged" and threatened that his followers may riot if he doesn't win.[68] Throughout the Republican primaries, Trump threatened the Republican

Party with destruction if they attempted to block his candidacy in any way, just as he has consistently attacked and threatened *Fox News*. The specter of a Republican Party candidate attacking the party that has nominated him and its chief media propaganda apparatus, *Fox News*, exhibits, I believe, an out of control malignant aggression and vengeful destructiveness syndrome.

Indeed, although Trump won the chaotic 2016 Republican Party primaries and was proclaimed their official party candidate, even after beating his maligned and deeply insulted opponents, Trump continued his defamations in even more destructive and offensive discourse. As Maureen Dowd pointed out Jeb Bush was "'a one day kill' as a gloating Trump put it, with the 'low energy' taunt. 'Liddle Marco' and 'Lyin' Ted' bit the dust. 'One-for-38 Kasich' fell by the wayside."[69] And after John Kasich refused to attend the Republican convention crowning Trump, even though it was held in a city in which he is governor, and after Ted Cruz told delegates to vote their consciences in the election, as a dig at Donald, a bitter Trump proclaimed on numerous weekend TV interviews after the convention that he was considering raising over ten million dollar funds to assure his Republican nemeses defeat in their next election campaigns.[70]

The extremely destructive behavior typical of Trump's entire campaign leads me to suggest that Fromm's analysis of the *"necrophilaic"* as an extreme form of malignant aggression also applies to Trump. Fromm illustrates the concept of the necrophilaic personality through an extensive study of Hitler as the paradigmatic of a highly destructive authoritarian personality, as he did a study of Himmler to illustrate his concept of the sadistic personality.[71] Fromm argues that the "necrophilaic transforms all life into things, including himself and the manifestations of his human faculties of reason, seeing, hearing, tasting, loving. Sexuality become a technical skill ("the love machine"); feelings are flattened and sometimes substituted for by sentimentality; joy, the expression of intense aliveness, is replaced by 'fun' or excitement; and whatever love and tenderness man has is directed toward machines and gadgets."[72]

In Fromm's analysis, the necrophilic personality type is fundamentally *empty,* needing to fill themselves with ever more acquisitions, conquests, or victories. Hence, it is no accident that the best single book on Trump by Michael D'Antonio is titled *Never Enough. Donald Trump and the Pursuit of Success*. Trump's need for adoration and his malignant and destructive rage at all criticism and opposition shows an extremely disordered personality who constitutes a grave danger to the United States and the world.

The necrophilic personality fills his emptiness with sadism, aggression, amassing wealth and power, and is prone to violence and self-destruction. Accounts of Trump's business dealings and entanglements with women show an incredible recklessness. When his first two marriages were unraveling, Trump carried out well-publicized affairs and seemed to revel in all the dirty publicity, no matter how demeaning. Likewise, in the 1990s when his business empire was spectacularly unravelling, Trump continued to make risky investments, put himself in impossible debt (with the help of banks who were taken in by his myth as a business man), and conned business associates, financial institutions and the public at large as he spiraled into near bankruptcy.[73]

Trump's destructive aspects are almost at the heart of his run for the presidency. Revealingly, Trump's initial "argument" for his presidency was to build a wall to keep immigrants from pouring over our southern border along with a promise to arrest all "illegal immigrants" and send them back over the border, a highly destructive (and probably impossible) action that would tear apart countless families. Trump promised to totally destroy ISIS and threatened to bring back waterboarding "and worse, much much worse!" he shouted repeatedly at his rallies and in interviews, although some Generals and military experts pointed out that Trump could not order troops or other citizens to break international law.

Hence, the peril and threats we face in a Trump presidency raises the issue of what does it mean to have an arguably sadistic, excessively narcissistic, malignantly aggressive, vengeably destructive, and necrophilic individual like Trump as president of the United States? If Trump indeed fits Fromm's criteria of the malignantly aggressive and necrophilic personality, this should be upsetting and raise some serious questions about Trump. Fromm was obsessed for decades about the danger of nuclear war and would no doubt be extremely disturbed at the thought of the Donald having his itchy finger on nuclear weapons launching. What would a foreign and domestic policy governed by a man with a malignant aggression syndrome look like?

At the end of his articulations of malignant aggression and necrophilia in *The Anatomy of Human Destructiveness* (1973), Fromm warned:

> It is hardly necessary to stress that severely necrophiluos persons are very dangerous. They are the haters, the racists, those in favor of war, bloodshed, and destruction. They are dangerous not only if they are political leaders, but also as the potential cohorts for a dictatorial leader. They become the executioners, terrorists, torturers; without them no terror system could be set up. But the less intense necrophiles are also politically important; while they may not be among the first adherents, they are necessary for the existence of a terror regime because they form a solid basis, although not necessarily a majority, for it to gain and hold power. (p. 368)

Hence, Frommian categories applied to Trump help illuminate why Donald Trump is so chaotic, dangerous, and destructive, and how risky it is to even contemplate Trump being President of the United States in these dangerous times. It is also worrisome to contemplate that Trump has developed a following through his demagoguery and that authoritarian populism constitutes a clear and present danger to U.S. democracy and an American Nightmare, that threatens world peace and global stability.

THE RESURRECTION OF RICHARD NIXON AND
AMERICAN NEO-FASCISM

During the month of June and early weeks of July, 2016, before the Republican National Convention in mid-July, the Trump campaign had a bad month. There was an unparalleled amount of high profile shooting of blacks by police and the emergence of Black Lives Matter and protests against police violence, followed by attacks by black men against police. On June 12, 2016, a 29-year-old security guard, who had pledged allegiance to ISIS, attacked a gay nightclub in Orlando Florida, went on a rampage and killed 49 people while wounding 53 others, in what was seen as the deadliest shooting against LGBT people in US history, as well as the deadliest terror attack since 9/11.

Trump took the occasion to brag that he was the one who had been warning about Islamic terror attacks, and reacted to the shooting by attacking presumptive Democratic nominee Hillary Clinton and President Obama, proclaiming: "In his remarks today, President Obama disgracefully refused to even say the words 'Radical Islam.' For that reason alone, he should step down. If Hillary Clinton, after this attack, still cannot say the two words 'Radical Islam' she should get out of this race for the presidency."

Hence, while the nation was mourning its loss, Trump continued his assaults on Muslims and touting himself as the only one who could protect the nation against such attacks. Throughout his 2016 campaign, Trump used the term *"the silent majority"* to describe his followers, a term Richard Nixon used to describe his white conservative followers who felt marginalized in the fierce racial, political, and cultural battles of the 1960s – a code word to appeal to aggrieved white voters.[74] To motivate and activate his followers, Trump arguably manipulates racism and nativism and plays to the sinister side of the American psyche and the long tradition of nationalism, America first-ism, and xenophobia, wanting to keep minorities and people of color in their place. Trump promotes himself as the tough guy that can stand up to the Russians and Chinese; he'll be the most militarist guy on the block and build up the US military, and allegedly make it again the major superpower.

In late June, Trump took a break from his campaign schedule to help inaugurate one of his son's new golf resorts in Scotland, while voters in the UK were deciding in a referendum on June 23 whether they should stay in the European Union or exit, in what came to be known as the "Brexit" referendum. Rightwing leaders played on fears of immigration and to extreme nationalism, both Trumpian motifs, and in a close vote chose to leave the UK, a result that pleased Trump who had supported the move which many saw as catastrophic for the UK and global economy (the markets plunged the next day, generating worries about the UK and global economy). Trump had been promoting an extreme nationalist and anti-immigrant agenda as the heart of his campaign from the beginning and it appears that this ideology has been global in impact.

With this background, Trump merged his "Make America Great Again" with aggressive taking up and promoting the slogan "America First" as a key component of his campaign. "America First" was the slogan of an anti-interventionist movement in the early 1940s to keep the US out of World War II that was associated with Charles Lindberg and American fascist and anti-Semitic forces.[75] Trump doesn't stress this connection but it serves as a dog-whistle to some of his extreme rightwing followers. As Libby Nelson points out: "Trump first showcased the term 'America First' in a foreign policy speech back in April, in which he declared that trade agreements, permanent alliances, and immigrants were burdens weakening America rather than the bonds that reinforce international peace."[76]

"'America First' will be the major and overriding theme of my administration," he said in his remarks after Brexit. To him, that meant disconnecting from other countries: more barriers to trade, tougher negotiations with longstanding allies in NATO, and a more restrictive immigration policy. Trump's "America First" discourse is thus an important part of his "Make America Great Again" discourse and links Trump's isolationism with his anti-NATO and pro-Putin discourse. Trump has continued to complain that the U.S. is paying too much of NATO's expenses and is prepared to dismantle the organization that has helped provide more than 60 years of European and American peace and prosperity after the two terrible World Wars of the twentieth century. Also disturbing is how Trump continues to speak favorably of his favorite authoritarian Maximum Leader Vladimir Putin – and has even made favorable remarks about Saddam Hussein who was "great at killing terrorists." Trump is obviously attracted to authoritarian dictators and makes it clear that he is prepared to be the U.S.'s Savior, Redeemer, and Maximum Problem Solver.

Trump promises to not only protect America from its foreign enemies but to protect his followers from dangerous and murderous forces at home. A few weeks after Brexit and Trump intensifying his America First motif, on July 5, 2016, Alton Sterling, a 37-year-old black man, was shot several times at while pinned to the ground by two white Baton Rouge police officers. The next day, on July 6, 2016, another black man Philando Castile was fatally shot by a police officer, in the suburbs of St. Paul Minnesota. Both events were caught on video, went viral and became media spectacles of police brutality, leading Black Lives Matter to stage nationwide protests. These shocking events were followed on July 7, 2016, by an angry Army Reserve black veteran of the Afghan wars ambushing and shooting at close range a group of police officers in Dallas, Texas, killing five officers and injuring nine others in the worst police massacre since 9/11.

In the aftermath of these eruptions of violence, Trump intensified his Nixonian Law and Order discourse, insisting he would get tough on crime and protect the country from the forces of disorder and anarchy. While President Obama and other national leaders were calling for calm and national unity, Trump continued to fan the flames of fear, hatred, and division, while promoting himself as the only one capable of solving the nation's decline and fall. These motifs were central to Trump's interventions in the Republican National Convention held in Cleveland from July 18–21, when Trump ascended to his proclaimed Coming Out as the Savior of the Nation.

THE REPUBLICAN NATIONAL CONVENTION AND
THE FACES OF AUTHORITARIAN POPULISM

Conventions provide four-day political info-mercials in which candidate and party can make their case and sell their product to the electorate. It provides an annual ritual in which party regulars can come together, hear speeches from party functionaries and favorites, debate platform issues, and unify and organize for the fall election.

Trump's convention was in no way typical. His followers were largely derived from his own rightwing populist movement and had contempt for the Republican Party regulars and elite. They were confronted with Ted Cruz's delegates who remainded fiercely loyal to Trump's one-time Bro become major nemesis. The third major GOP contender, Ohio Governor John Kasisch, who was Governor of the state in which the convention was held, refused to come or support Trump. Also boycotting the convention with the Bush Family were previous GOP presidential candidates Mitt Romney and John McCain, and many Republican Senators, Congressmen, and functionaries who found Donald Trump totally repellant, refused to support him, and wanted nothing to do with him.

Bikers for Trump, however, were there in full force regalia, promising to protect Trump supporters from protestors, who, surprisingly turned out in small numbers and were kept far from the convention area. Hence, the chaos expected at the Republican convention was confined to within the aptly named Quicken Loans Arena, evidently owned by a Mortgage Committee, appropriate for a builder whose agenda promised to mortgage the whole country to pay for the outlandish agenda outlined in Trump's bombastic stump speeches and promises to build a wall across Mexico, build up the military, create jobs, and make America great again.

Trump's arrival followed the scenario of the Nazi *Triumph of the Will* spectacle that marked many of his southern rallies. The media and a crowd of designated delegates waited anxiously as the Trump Jet flew into Cleveland, whirling around the airport before landing to make sure of good pictures. After landing, the Trump entourage entered a helicopter to fly to the convention center where Mike Pence and his family and chosen delegates were invited to meet him. After an awkward attempt to greet Pence with a big smacky New York kiss, the Indiana Governor turned away with horror and the embarrassing moment was quickly erased with a manly handshake. The Trump and Pence families posed together for pictures, then went marching toward the convention center with the media in tow, trying to catch every possible frame of the spectacle.

RNC DAY 1: CHAOS IN THE HALL, FEAR AND HATE, AND MELANIA'S PLAGIARISM

Day One of the Republican National Convention in Cleveland was marked at its opening by a clash involving rowdy debates among delegates who wanted a change of rules so that delegates wouldn't be bound by their state primary results and delegates allowed to vote their conscience and thus presumably vote against Trump. The Colorado delegation was especially outspoken, and although it appeared their motion was carried by the convention Yeah/Nay vote, they found the convention Chair ruling against the delegation and later awarding all their delegate votes to Trump – although Cruz had won in most of the caucuses, leading the Colorado delegate to leave the floor – and confirming Trump's claim during the primaries that the system was rigged, although this time his gang was doing the rigging.

The convention opened with initial speeches which took an apocalyptic gloom and doom tone with hysterical tirades about how horrible the United States and its place in the world was under the Obama administration and what a disaster it would be to elect Hillary Clinton to continue the Downfall of the Republic. Former New York Mayor Rudi Giuliani was especially hysterical screeching out a tirade against Obama and Clinton which previewed Trump's unhinged rant. Presentations were focused on the 2012 Benghazi, Libya attack that had killed Ambassador Chris Stevens and other Americans, and a distraught mother blamed Hillary Clinton, who was Secretary of State at the time, overlooking that the President, Secretary of Defense, Pentagon, and National Security Team take such responsibility.

The highlight of the first evening unfolded with Trump walking through a door bathed in blue light and entering the auditorium, like God magically appearing through the primordial mists to bequeath his blessing on all the followers. He introduced in short remarks his wife Melana who proceeded to give one of the few speeches of the dreary evening that showed class and reason. Commentators agreed with many in the audience that Melania Trump made a poised and appealing pitch for her husband in what was taken as one of the best speeches of the convention. While delegates and TV commentators were agreed that she'd hit a "grand-slam home run," minutes after the conclusion of the convention Day One, the media revealed that a blogger had discovered that there were paragraphs lifted from a 2008 convention speech by Michelle Obama.

Melania's plagiarism soon became the most discussed theme of the Republican convention and continued to dominate media chatter for the next three days. While the media played over and over passages where Melania quotes Michelle word for word, Trump's campaign manager Paul Manafort, and many Trump surrogates, denied that there was plagiarism and claimed that it was sheer coincidence that there were word for word repetitions, even though the obvious plagiarisms were played over and over on TV and cited in the press, such as a *Washington Post* entry that set the paragraphs in question side by side.

Michelle Obama speech in 2008	*Melania Trump speech in 2016*
"And Barack and I were raised with so many of the same values: that you work hard for what you want in life; that your word is your bond and you do what you say you're going to do; that you treat people with dignity and respect, even if you don't know them, and even if you don't agree with them."	"From a young age, my parents impressed on me the values that you work hard for what you want in life, that your word is your bond and you do what you say and keep your promise, that you treat people with respect. They taught and showed me values and morals in their daily lives. That is a lesson that I continue to pass along to our son."
"And Barack and I set out to build lives guided by these values, and pass them on to the next generation."	"And we need to pass those lessons on to the many generations to follow."
"Because we want our children – and all children in this nation – to know that the only limit to the height of your achievements is the reach of your dreams and your willingness to work for them."	"Because we want our children in this nation to know that the only limit to your achievements is the strength of your dreams and your willingness to work for them."[77]

Hence, Day 1 of the convention opened with a Never-Trump insurrection that was crushed by the Republican establishment running the convention which exploded into chaos on the floor during the first few hours, followed at the conclusion by accusations of Melania Trump's plagiarism, a motif that dominated media coverage for the next three days, until the Trump organization admitted that one of the speechwriters accidentally inscribed words from a speech by Michelle Obama which Melania inserted into her own speech, without proper attribution.[78]

The two-day denial of Melania's plagiarism by the Trump organization, led by Paul Manafort, revealed the continuation of a post-Truth Republican regime that replicated the contempt for truth in the Bush-Cheney administration. Karl Rove and others in the Bush-Cheney administration regularly lied and aggressively attacked the media when criticized for lying, thus institutionalizing post-truth discourse which Trump would take up with gusto.[79]

RNC DAY 2: SEXISM AMOK, BULLSHIT, AND THE DEMONIZATION OF HILLARY CLINTON

Melana's plagiarism continued to dominate the news cycle with Paul Manafort and other Trump surrogates continuing to aggressively deny that plagiarism ever took place and with Manafort blaming the story on Hillary Clinton and her tendency to try to destroy strong women – a vulgar and vicious attack that revealed Manafort's truly reptilian nature.

Manafort was touted to the media when he became head of Trump's presidential campaign as a Republican insider and adviser to the presidential campaigns of Republicans Gerald Ford, Ronald Reagan, George H. W. Bush, Bob Dole, George W. Bush, and John McCain, but he is better known as a lobbyist for a group of Third World thugs (some of whom I noted above). Throughout the day, Manafort continued to deny Melania's plagiarism, and never apologized for his blatant lying, revealing the Trump campaign proclivity for Nixonian stone-walling and Bush-Cheney Big, Bold, and Brazen Lies.

All major Trump biographies account that Trump's lying is epic and grandiose, and *The Guardian* has a weekly account of Trump's lies, while the *Washington Post* frequently documents them. Fareed Zakaria suggested on CNN in early August, 2016, that Trump is as much a classic bullshitter as liar, in the sense of philosophy professor Harry Frankfurt's concept of bullshit, and defined Trump in good old New York street lingo as a "bullshit artist."[80] By summer 2016, the non-partisan website PolitiFact rated 78% of Trump's campaign trail claims as Mostly False, False, or Pants on Fire, highlighting the mixture of fact and falsity which constitutes bullshit.[81] Crucially, Frankfurt distinguishes between lies and bullshit, arguing: "Telling a lie is an act with a sharp focus. It is designed to insert a particular falsehood at a specific point. In order to invent a lie at all, the teller of a lie must think he knows what is true. But someone engaging in BS is neither on the side of the true nor on the side of the false, his eyes not on the facts at all." While a liar knows the truth and takes pains to misrepresent it convincingly, a bullshitter casually mixes fact and fiction because, for him, the truth is beside the point. Trump is the epitome of a Frankfurtian bullshitter in that his rhetoric functions primarily to manipulate his audience in the moment and the hypernarcissist Trump assumes that everything he says is true.

During his entire life, bullshit artist Donald J. Trump mixed hyperbole and falsehood in talking about his businesses, his wives, his buildings, his books, and even how his many business failures and bankruptcies were "great," because they always allowed him to come out ahead. More disturbingly, while perpetrating the "birther" myth that Barack Obama was born in Kenya, Trump insisted that he had private investigators in Hawaii who had unearthed amazing documents that proved Obama wasn't born in the U.S., and Trump never apologized for his birther campaign. Playing on his audiences' Islamophobia after a strong of terrorist attacks in Summer 2016, Trump claimed repeatedly that he saw New Jersey Muslims celebrating the fall of the World Trade Center on 9/11. Knowing that his Know-Nothing rightwing audiences do not believe in climate change, Trump shamelessly repeats climate denier rhetoric and repeats discredited claims that vaccines cause autism just to manipulate his audience into thinking he is one of them. Yet sometimes Donald's bullshit stems from base ignorance and a tendency to be a Know-It-All who just can't get his big mouth shut.

The Republican convention itself was dedicated to the bashing and demonizing of Hillary Rodham Clinton. Speaker after speaker attacked Clinton, focusing on her damned email-scandal that had been a major theme of the summer and her role in the Benghazi fiasco which had been the subject of an eight hour Congressional hearing in which she emerged unscathed. Yet the Republicans insisted on replaying every gruesome incident of the 2012 Benghazi death of the popular U.S. Ambassador Christopher Stevens, including a bereaved mother lamenting her son's death in tears and shrieks and blaming Clinton for her son's death.

RNC DAY 3: MELANIA'S PLAGIARISM REVEALED, THE RESURRECTION OF RICHARD NIXON, AND THE TREACHERY OF TED CRUZ

The news cycle of Day Three of the convention began with a confession by the Trump Campaign that a speech writer/employee of the Trump organization had indeed worked with Melania on her speech and inadvertently wrote the plagiarized text into the speech when Melania read over the phone some passage from a speech from Michele Obama, but the Trump campaign insisted that no one would be fired, although the employee had offered her resignation.[82] As TV commentators continued to indicate through the day, someone above the hapless employee, however, should have taken responsibility for the plagiarism, as usually campaigns carefully vet their speeches to make sure that there are not embarrassing errors. Moreover, for the past two days Paul Manafort and other Trumpsters had aggressively insisted that there was no plagiarism, revealing the spokespeople of the Trump campaign as liars and hypocrites who modify their party line from moment to moment and follow the Nixonian practice of "stonewalling" when it suits their interests. It also revealed the rank amateurism of the Trump campaign (dis)organization that had allowed the Melania plagiarism story to dominate the news cycle for the first three days of the Republican convention, displaying a spectacle of rubes and cons who didn't know how to run a TV convention and get a coherent message across. Hardly any speaker had made a compelling case for the election of Donald Trump and the celebrities and "entertainment" that Donald Trump had promised turned out to be C-list celebrity has-beens, and the entertainment was largely blaring live rock music and the chaos provided by the disorganized convention.

It was becoming clear that Trump's campaign was following the strategy and trajectory of the 1968 campaign of Richard Nixon. At a Bloomberg News breakfast, on the first morning of the convention, Paul Manafort had told reporters to take a look at Richard Nixon's 1968 acceptance speech, suggesting the parallels with Trump and saying that the Trump campaign found inspiration there. Indicating that the campaign was studying past convention speeches, they focused on Nixon's 1968 acceptance speech in Miami, Florida. Trump had said to a New York Times reporter: "I think what Nixon understood is that when the world is falling apart, people want a strong leader whose highest priority is protecting America first. The sixties were bad, really bad. And it's really bad now. Americans feel like it's chaos again." Manafort insisted that Nixon's speech "is pretty much on line with a lot of the issues that are going on today."

Since the shootings of policeman by black men in Dallas and Baton Rouge in early July, Trump was highlighting as a major theme that he was "the law and order candidate," a theme taken up by Nixon in 1968 (ironically Nixon's Vice President Spiro Agnew ended up going to jail for corruption and Nixon was the first president to resign while in office during the Watergate affair, fair warning to the public not to be taken in by law and order demagogues).

Trump, like Nixon and Agnew, attacked the media, banning newspapers like *The Washington Post* from covering his events, and attacking reporters that criticize him. At his rallies in summer of 2016 Trump encouraged his campaign crowds to boo and hiss at the reporters covering him, and regularly personally insulted in vulgar terms particular journalists who gain his ire. Likewise, Nixon had Agnew tour the nation assaulting television and news media, which his operative Pat Buchanan once labelled the "nattering nabobs of negativism". Trump used as well invective-filled tweets aimed at any journalist who wrote an unflattering story about him, bringing to mind Agnew regularly calling out individual reporters by name in those same speeches.

Just as Nixon had his "enemies list" and Attorney General John Mitchell to persecute and harass his "enemies" in different ways, Trump called on N.J. Governor and former federal prosecutor Chris Christie to attack Trump critics as well as to "prosecute" Hillary Clinton. Touted as a prospective attorney general in a Trump administration, Christie promised Trump would purge Obama-appointed federal employees and would prosecute Hillary Clinton if he became president. And in the realm of foreign policy, just as Nixon claimed in the 1968 presidential campaign that he had a "secret plan" to end the Vietnam war (that never materialized), so too does Trump have a "secret plan" to destroy ISIS.

Indeed, Nixon's law-and-order theme was developed in an aggressive way on Day Two of the Republican national Convention, as New Jersey Governor Chris Christie, one of Trump's most high-profile Establishment supporters promised to "prosecute" Hillary Clinton and proceeded to list her most prominent "crimes," followed by a call-and-shout by the "jury" at the convention, who shrieked "Guilty!" as Christie listed her supposed crimes. Soon, however, the blood-thirsty Republican crowd chanted louder and louder "lock her up." Indeed, the "lock her up" theme began to surface as the most popular theme of the frenzied Republican mob, revealing their sexism and desire to control and even destroy strong women.

As Adele Stan points out: "Much of the [second] night was devoted to demonizing Clinton. Of all people, New Jersey Governor Chris Christie was chosen to make the case 'as a former federal prosecutor' for why the Democratic presumptive nominee is guilty of crimes and shenanigans. This, just days after Christie's own close confidante, David Samson, pleaded guilty before a federal judge to one count of bribery for, as Salon's Robert Hennelly put it, "shaking down United Airlines in his role as chairman of the Port Authority of New York & New Jersey, a position to which Christie appointed him. Not to mention the indictments of Christie's aides in the Bridgegate scandal."[83]

Trump himself had introduced this theme early in his campaign as he repeatedly insisted that "Crooked Hillary" should go to jail for her alleged crimes, although the FBI chief himself reported in a July 6 news conference by F.B.I. Director James B. Comey that there were no grounds upon which to prosecute Clinton.[84] Adele Stan notes the "witch-burning" tone of the convention and atavistic desire to prosecute and destroy Hillary Clinton. Ben Carson, an early challenger to Trump for the rightwing vote in the primaries, tried to associate Clinton with Lucifer, by means of her contact with Saul Alinksy who ironically dedicated his book *Rules for Radicals* to Lucifer, "the first radical," and with whom Hillary Clinton had corresponded, thus in Carson's tortured logic associating her with Lucifer himself!

Going one step further, Al Baldasaro, a New Hampshire state representative and Trump advisor on military affairs, said of Clinton on a radio interview: "She is a disgrace for the lies that she told those mothers about their children that got killed over there in Benghazi. This whole thing disgusts me, Hillary Clinton should be put in the firing line and shot for treason."[85] As during his campaign, Trump had incited his followers to violence in word and deed, and he would continue to in the days following.

The chaos and disorder in the convention continued in Day Three when the Trump Campaign scheduled Ted Cruz to provide a prime time speech just before Vice-President designate Mike Pence's effort to sell the Trump candidacy and himself as a loyal Vice-President to more mainstream Republicans. Cruz went rogue, however, going well over his allotted time, and rather than endorsing Trump, Cruz told voters to follow their conscience and in effect vote for whomever they like, leading to an outburst of booing. Cruz joked that he "appreciated the enthusiasm of the New York delegation" that stood up and loudly booed him, setting off an eruption of booing throughout the auditorium. The Trump campaign had received Cruz's speech in advance and Donald Trump walked onto the convention floor just as Cruz was finishing leading to shouts of "Trump, Trump, Trump," as the Maximum Leader attracted the focus of the TV camera which would invariably focus on the Orange-Haired Demi-God who absorbed emanations of the camera and translated them into images and spectacles that dominated the TV screens and consciousness of Trump's Coronation and thrilled his frenzied acolytes.

It appeared that Ted Cruz had never forgiven Trump for tweeting unflattering pictures of Cruz's wife Heidi in the course of the campaign, while threatening to "spill the beans" on her. Nor had he forgiven Trump's smear that Cruz's father Rafael was involved in the Kennedy Assassination, a fantastic claim that made clear that there was no limit to Trump's ability to smear, besmirch, and generate the most outrageous lies imaginable (God knows what he has stored up for Hillary). Cruz got his revenge by accepting Trump's invitation to speak at the convention, to give a spell-binding speech punctuated by explosions of standing ovations, concluding with Cruz dumping a big turd on the stage in the form of a refusal to endorse Trump, stating: "Please, don't stay home in November. Stand, and speak, and vote your conscience, vote for candidates up and down the ticket who you trust to defend our freedom and to be faithful to the constitution."

Cruz's intervention disrupted any fantasy of unity in the party and spoiled the atmosphere for the speeches of Mike Pence and Eric Trump, with all media buzz focused on Ted Cruz's audacious self-promotion at the expense of Donald Trump and Republican Party unity. Pence's speech was especially boring and got almost no media attention, as Ted Cruz stole the news cycles and media commentators insisted Trump must hit a grand-slam home run in his speech the final day to keep the convention from becoming a total disaster. So far, hardly anyone had gotten across the message of why anyone should vote for Donald Trump, with most of the airtime going to trashing Hillary Clinton, or promoting the mediocre speakers assembled in a convention marked by what will probably be remembered as one of the worst-organized and uninspiring conventions of modern times.

RNC DAY 4: THE RED FACED ORANGE MAN RANTS

Day 4 began with buzz concerning whether Donald Trump could pull off a speech that would unify and mobilize the convention and impress viewers at home that Trump was worthy of their vote. Results were mixed. His daughter Ivanka pleasingly introduced Trump as a great dad and boss, but did not really touch on any political issues. Trump himself then took center stage, behind a specially installed gold and black lectern with giant letters 15-feet high spelling TRUMP standing above him, as he glared at the audience and camera and blared out the

Shakespearean opening line that associated him with Julius Caesar: "Friends, delegates and fellow Americans: I humbly and gratefully accept your nomination for the presidency of the United States."

No doubt Trump was blissfully unaware that he was appropriating the lines of Mark Anthony's funeral oration after Caesar's assassination, but the rest of the frightening speech made clear that Trump envisaged himself as another Caesar. A grim-faced Trump stared relentlessly at the teleprompter throughout his 75-minute dirge on the decline of America and its impending collapse, and dutifully read his doleful words, pronouncing each slowly and carefully, managing to shout out the entire speech without his usual manic asides. Trump's stare and lack of animation made him appear more comic-book caricature than usual, although the content of the speech was the crazed rant of a fanatic authoritarian populist, as Trump enumerated all the dangers to the nation, highlighting a wave of domestic crime, that he blamed on immigrants, enumerating in detail some grizzly examples in which undocumented immigrants committed heinous crimes, followed by the usual Islamophobia and dangers of Muslims pouring into the country and committing acts of terrorism, to which his audience chanted "build the wall! Build the wall!"

Trump repeated at least four time that he was the *Law and Order* candidate and also gestured to his America First motif, punctuated inevitably by his Stormtroopers changing "USA! USA! USA!" After the gloom and doom vision of a declining America and a rigged system, Trump declared in Fuhrer-fashion that: "I alone can fix it." Hence, his crowd was led to believe he, Donald J. Trump, – a self-proclaimed billionaire who has bankrupted many companies, defaulted on bank loans, failed to pay contractors for service, and who was the very epitome of capitalist greed, – was going to fix the system and serve the people. Further, this shouting red-faced demagogue claimed that he was the "voice of the forgotten men and women" – a Depression era phrase of the Roosevelt administration which Trump inflects toward his white constituency who believes they have been forgotten and passed over in favor of privileged elites and favored minorities.

Conservative commentators on the networks like Hugh Hewitt on CNN praised the speech, as did former KKK grand wizard David Duke who, inspired by Trump, was running for the Senate in Louisiana. In the most brazen lie of the night, Trump proclaimed that: "Here at our convention, there will be no lies." Of course, Trump's speech was full of the usual lies and the next day *The Guardian*, *The Washington Post*, and other fact checkers pointed out that crime was actually down, that Trump had exaggerated the extent of crime that was committed by undocumented workers, and used many outdated statistics.[86] Moreover, his claim was obviously bogus that: "the crime and violence that today afflicts our nation will soon – and I mean very soon – come to an end. Beginning on January 20th of 2017, safety will be restored" – by Donald J. Trump! Again, Trump is projecting a demagogic image of a Superman that will instantly solve all problems, without giving any concrete proposals for how that will happen.

Like Richard Nixon, Trump played on his audience's fear of crime and violence, but grossly exaggerated crime figures and made his case with grizzly examples of crimes by immigrants, mixed with reminders of recent acts of terrorism in the U.S. and Europe, thus manipulating his followers' emotions who watched his grim recitation of doom and gloom in rapt attention with tears showing flowing down the faces of some of the convention audience. Trump was the vox populi of his follower's fears and rage and humiliations, and the orange-haired red-faced demagogue presented himself as the only hope for America, and the only one who could solve the problems he dramatized. Like previous 20th century demagogues, Trump promised he would "Make America Great Again," and his followers burst into an ecstatic chant of "USA! USA! USA!" every time Trump evoked the return to the Golden Age that Trump promised would return.

Looking at the largely white faces in the convention, it was clearer than ever that Trump was primarily addressing the fears and issues of alienated white people, and there was little reaching out to minorities and people of color, or even of faith -except a thank you to evangelicals for their support, which he admitted he didn't deserve. Breaking with Republican homophobia or benign neglect ("Don't Ask, Don't Tell"), the red-faced man gave a shout out to gays and lesbians, even though his party platform was homophobic to the core, as was his Vice-President pick Mike Pence, who had signed a "religious liberty" law in

Indiana that enabled businesses not to have to sell to gays and lesbians or anyone that contravened their religious beliefs.

And while in the past Trump has been more entertaining and even genial, in Cleveland the dominant emotion he conveyed was rage. As Jennifer Ruben put it: "His face contorted, his face glistening with sweat and his voice bellowing for long portions of the speech, he seemed every bit the image of a dictator of another era. Only his bright-orange-ish makeup reminded us this was not a grainy black-and-while newsreel capturing a master of manipulation from Europe in the 1930s or a segregationist governor in the South in the 1960s, but the high-def picture of a modern demagogue."[87]

Trump concluded his 75 minute rant by claiming his political philosophy was unified by the theme of putting America First, shouting: "To all Americans tonight, in all our cities and towns, I make this promise: we will make America strong again. We will make America proud again. We will make America safe again and we will make America great again." Note that all Trump makes is a "promise" without any details and his usual response when someone asks him how he will accomplish his goals, is, "I'll get it done! Believe me! Believe me!"

Indeed, "Believe me!" is the revealing sign of an authoritarian demagogue who wants his followers to except his promises as binding and his Word as the Truth to which they must submit. From the beginning of his campaign, Trump has asked his followers to believe he would build The Great Wall of Trump along the southern border, would create Trumpian "deportation forces" to arrest and send back to their places of origin the at least 11 million immigrants without papers, that he would Make America Safe and Great, and that he alone could do it. Now Trump must convince the country that He is the One in the hard fought campaign that would follow.

THE DOG DAYS OF SUMMER: THE DEMS CONVENE AND TRUMP IMPLODES

The Republican convention was judged a "big hot mess" by many critics,[88] and Trump's speech was seen as overly pessimistic, uninspiring, and poorly delivered, playing on the rage and fear that motivated many who came to Trump's rallies, but not to mainstream Republicans. The Democrats convention, by contrast, was appraised a success. After a rocky start, in which Bernie Sanders' followers booed Hillary Clinton and even Bernie himself when he endorsed Clinton and told his followers in "the real world," she is the alternative to Donald Trump. Sanders also insisted that his forces had pushed the Democrats to approve the most progressive platform in party history.

The first night of the Democratic National Convention was "progressive night" with a dramatic speech by Michelle Obama, followed by a passionate presentation by liberal icon Elizabeth Warren, and a fiery talk by Sanders who again endorsed Clinton and made the case why she was far superior to Trump. The Dems' slogan was "Stronger Together," and in the following days the party appeared unified and enthusiastic to hear their Party Stars like Barack Obama, Joe Biden, and Bill Clinton make the case for Hillary Clinton and bash Trump. While Trump had promised to get top celebrities and entertainers to make the Republican convention spectacular entertainment, he failed miserably in getting any celebrities, settling for a C-list ex-sit com bit player and soap opera actor, while the Democrats got Meryl Streep, Sarah Silverman and Al Franken who did an effective comedy routine, and a series of popular singers and musicians.

The Dems also mobilized ex-generals, diplomats, and military families to endorse Clinton and indicate the dangers of a Trump presidency for national security. One memorable appearance involved the Khans, a Muslim "Gold Star" family who had lost their son in Afghanistan, who sacrificed his life to save his comrades. When the father excoriated Trump, saying he did not know the meaning of "sacrifice" and that his anti-Muslim ban would not have permitted the family to enter the country, Trump fired back with a series of tweets attacking the Khans and appeared on TV the next day insisting that he had performed many sacrifices in building up his real estate empire.

More astonishing, in a much-discussed aftermath of the Democratic National convention, Trump continued to attack the Khan family, that had lost its son in military service and testified to their loss and disgust at Trump's attacks on Muslims at a much-discussed moment in the Democratic National Convention. Trump tweeted a nasty attack on the grieving mother who had stood as a silent witness beside her husband, and whose silence he attacked as evidence that Muslims didn't let women speak in public. Trump's attacks on the Khan family continued for days after the convention and major Republicans distanced themselves from Trump's rancorous and vile comments.

Continuing to shock the Republican establishment, Trump proclaimed on August 2 that he was not endorsing Republican House Leader Paul Ryan, former Presidential candidate John McCain, and others who had criticized him, thus threatening to blow apart the Republican Party – driving Party leaders to declare that they were staging an "intervention" with Trump over the weekend to try to persuade their candidate to act more "presidential" and to stop attacking Republican leaders – a gesture his base seems to love.[89]

Demonstrating Trump's deeply rooted and uncontrollable malignant aggression, Trump had what observers saw as the worst week of his campaign in early August as he continued to malign the Khan family, praised Vladimir Putin and called on the Russian strongman to hack Hillary Clinton's email, refused until the last moment to endorse fellow Republicans Ryan and McCain, threw a crying baby and its mother out of one of his rallies, and continued to make crazy off-the-cuff remarks. Topping off his going over the top, on August 9, 2016 in a rally at Wilmington, North Carolina, Trump appeared to suggest that gun rights supporters might take matters into their own hands if Hillary Clinton is elected President and appoints Judges who favor stricter gun control measures. Repeating the lie that Clinton wanted to abolish the right to bear arms, Trump warned that: "If she gets to pick her judges, nothing you can do, folks," Mr. Trump said, as the crowd began to boo. He quickly added: "Although the Second Amendment people – maybe there is, I don't know."

Some members of the audience visibly winced and for the next several days the news cycle was dominated by discussion that Trump had suggested that "Second Amendment" people (i.e. gun owners) might have to take the law into their own hands if Clinton was elected, raising the specter of political assassination and reminding people of the wave of political assassinations in the 1960s of JFK, RFK, and Martin Luther King, and assassination attempts against Presidents Gerald Ford and Ronald Reagan. Democrats, gun control advocates, and others, accused Trump of possibly inciting violence against Hillary Clinton or liberal Justices. Bernice A. King, daughter of the Rev. Dr. Martin Luther King Jr., called Mr. Trump's words "distasteful, disturbing, dangerous," and many other prominent citizens denounced Trump's dangerous rabble-rousing as further evidence that he was not fit to be President of the United States.[90]

As usual, Trump and his surrogates spun Trump's statements and attacked the media for twisting his meaning, and other Republicans like Paul Ryan dismissed it as a bad joke, but it was clear that this was further evidence that Trump was seriously unbalanced and highly dangerous, a genuine American Nightmare.

The Democrats pulled ahead about five points after their national convention and ten-fifteen points ahead during the first weeks in August as Trump continued to attack Republican leaders, ramble incoherently at his rallies, and defended Putin in interviews, even encouraging the Russians to hack Hillary Clinton and release emails that had allegedly disappeared from her days at the State Department. Pundits attacked Trump's ignorance about foreign affairs, when in an interview with *ABC News* he insisted Russia would not invade the Crimea, the interviewer had to tell Trump they already had. Trump confused Democratic Vice President candidate Tim Kane, the Governor of Virginia, with Thomas Keane, the governor of New Jersey, evidently not paying any attention to what the Democrats were doing. It was becoming clear that Trump was a Know Nothing, who had no policy positions, grasp of the issues, or knowledge of the dynamics of U.S. politics and history.

AUGUST ANTICS AND TRUMPSTER CHAOS

The first week in August 2016 saw numerous articles claiming that Trump's campaign and perhaps his mind was unraveling, that he might not even make it through the next 90-plus days of the campaign, and even that he was plain crazy.[91] Trump had taken to calling Clinton the "devil" and chiding Bernie Sanders for making a "deal with the devil." Secretary Clinton was also, according to Trump, along with Barack Obama, "the founder of ISIS," and whenever he described her as "crooked Hillary," the enraptured crowd chanted "lock her up," with Trump smiling and encouraging his minions. In a classic case of projection, in a stump speech on August 5, Trump proclaimed that Hillary Clinton, "the Queen of Corruption," was "pretty close to unhinged and you've seen it…she is like an unbalanced person." Predicting the "destruction of this country from within" if Clinton is elected as the president, Trump was obviously following his handlers' advice to stick to attacking Clinton and not fellow Republicans as he slowly read his diatribe from a prepared speech that he held in his small hands.

As Trump's poll numbers nationally and in key swing states continued to plummet in August, Crazy Donald returned to his primary theme that "the election is rigged" – a claim Trump makes whenever he is behind in his beloved polls. While campaigning in Philadelphia, Trump charged that election rigging was especially likely in African American precincts and called on his followers to "monitor" polling places, raising the specter that Trump was calling on his troops to intimidate black voters and would claim a stolen election if Clinton won, unleashing his rabid hell hounds to protest.

During the week of August 15, rumors flew that Roger Ailes, long the President of *Fox News* who was deeply connected with Republican politics, was going to run Trump's campaign, or at least to be his debate coach for the coming Presidential debates that were sometimes considered to be the key event of the presidential election cycle. Ailes had just been fired from *Fox News* after a lawsuit was filed against him for sexual harassment, and many more *Fox News* women employees claimed that they too were sexually harassed by Ailes. Then, the morning of August 17, the Trump campaign announced the appointment of former investment banker Stephen Bannon, currently the executive chairman of Breitbart News, to become his campaign manager. The hardright website *Breitbart News* had been one of Trump's most ferocious supporters that fed on Trump's most extreme nationalist, racist, xenophobic, Islamophobic, and aggressive instincts and tendency to promote the most extreme conspiracy theories and extremist ideas, a feature of both Trump and the Breitbart site. Indeed, Bannon was characterized by news sources as the "most dangerous political operative in America",[92] as well as well as "the Leni Riefenstahl of the Tea Party movement,"[93] referring to films he'd made celebrating Sarah Palin and the Tea Party, and vilifying the Clintons and Obama, portending an even nastier and dirtier Trump campaign.

These appointments suggested that during the last weeks of the campaign "Trump will be Trump" and his most aggressive instincts would be unleashed, that there would be no "lid on the Id" as one Republican operative ruefully mourned. With Ailes and Bannon, Trump would have two of the most hard right and hardball political operatives imaginable by his side, with Nixon era Dirty Trickster Roger Stone lurking in the background, and with no one knowing to what extremes the Trump campaign will go.[94]

Curiously, the funder of *Breitbart News*, Robert Mercer, was becoming one of Trump's major funders, while its' ideologue-in-chief Steve Bannon was brought in to help run Trump's campaign. This is ironic since *Breitbart News* – in addition to promoting wild conspiracy theorists and racist, sexist and Islamophobic rants – has been dedicated to destroying the Republican Party elite. Emerging from the far-right fringes of the Tea Party, *Breitbart* helped produce a toxic "alt-right" blogosphere which curiously focused more hate and venom on the Republican establishment than on Democrats. Their first target was Republican House leader Eric Cantor who made the catastrophic mistake of discussing amnesty for immigrants with the Obama administration and was subject to vicious attack by *Breitbart* and the lunatic right. The extreme right found a kindred Republican radical to run against Cantor, and with *Breibart* leading the charge, the Virginia Congressman lost his 2010 Congressional primary. *Breitbart* next hounded House Speaker John Boehner to resign, and went after Paul Ryan, in a crusade to take down the House Republican leadership. Hence, the Trump campaign was now being funded and advised by alt-right figures hell-bent on destroying the Republican Party.[95]

Meanwhile, constitutional law scholars claimed that Trump's call for "extreme vetting" of immigrants, including a screening process to root out applicants who do not uphold "American values," was unconstitutional as well as "un-American."[96] Smacking of McCarthyism and the Cold War, Trump's extreme position on immigration was so obviously far out of the mainstream that he was forced to "pivot." Further, Trump had threatened an attack on the free press and constitutional law in a speech in Fort Worth, Texas in February where he said:

> One of the things I'm going to do if I win, and I hope we do and we're certainly leading. I'm going to open up our libel laws so when they write purposely negative and horrible and false articles, we can sue them and win lots of money. We're going to open up those libel laws. So when *The New York Times* writes a hit piece which is a total disgrace or when *The Washington Post*, which is there for other reasons, writes a hit piece, we can sue them and win money instead of having no chance of winning because they're totally protected... We're going to open up libel laws, and we're going to have people sue you like you've never got sued before.[97]

Carrying out libel suits against newspapers would contravene a tradition of freedom of the press set by *New York Times Co. v. Sullivan* which was decided by the Supreme Court in 1964, and established the right of the press to publish critical articles n politicians and public figures, unless intentional malice could be proved. Trump, of course, has been manipulating throughout his campaign rightwing distrust of the establishment press, but never before has a presidential candidate threatened to curtail freedom of the press, or ban certain publications that criticize him from rallies and public events.

65

Over the weekend of August 20, Trump met with Latino leaders in Trump Towers, and during the next week there was speculation that Trump was going to "soften" his position on immigration, leading his extremist followers like Ann Coulter and Sarah Palin to threaten Trump that he would lose his base if he modified his hardline position on immigration that was the core issue for many of his rabid supporters. Yet it was becoming increasingly obvious to the small rational core within the Trump campaign that it was impossible to round up and deport as many as 11 million illegal immigrants, and that deploying what Trump called "deportation squads" to break up families, incarcerate millions, and unleash the dogs of racial hate and perhaps war would all end badly.

After meeting with Latinos and telling them that he wanted every one of their votes, Trump turned to African Americans and told them that he was the One to solve all their problems and overcome their multiple oppressions and miseries. After enumerating the terrible poverty, jobs, education and community situation of African Americans, where "you cannot go down the street without getting shot," Trump assured the black population that he would protect and save them after the Democrats had obviously failed to help them. Not surprisingly, African Americans were not so trusting or grateful that Trump would be their champion, remembering how Donald and his father Fred were federally investigated for redlining and taking measures not to rent their properties to blacks, remembering that Donald Trump in effect called for the lynching of the "Central Park Five," young African Americans accused of raping a white girl in Central Park (it turned out they were innocent), and, oh yes, it was Donald Trump who was the original Birther, claiming that the first African American president, Barack Obama, was born in Kenya.[98]

After "pivoting" to a kinder and gentler Donald Trump, who pundits claimed was trying to scrape up some votes from Republican white, suburban women, appalled by Trump's bigotry and crassness, he went back to his old racist stunts. Showing that his heart and soul were really on the extreme right, Trump invited anti-EU and Brexit leader Nigel Farage to join him for a rally in Mississippi on August 24. In the heart of southern racist darkness, Trump shouted out: "Hillary

Clinton is a bigot!" while Farage assured his deep-south American cousins that he "wouldn't vote for Clinton if you paid me," and not surprisingly no one offered the Brit hate-monger a farthing. Hillary Clinton decried Trump's campaign strategy of embracing racism and racial tension, and hit back sharply in a late-night phone interview on CNN, charging: "[Trump] is taking a hate movement mainstream... He's brought it into his campaign. He is bringing it to our communities and our country."

The next day, Clinton presented in a speech in Reno, Nevada, a succinct and pointed summary of what she described as Donald Trump's "long history of racial discrimination." Clinton started by recalling the federal charges against Trump's discriminatory renting practices against people of color back in the 1980s to the 2008 Trump's promoting the "birther" attack on Barack Obama up to Trump's current campaign. Clinton argued that Trump was advancing a "racist ideology" which she claimed was bringing hate groups into the mainstream of U.S. politics. Clinton's coup de grace highlighted the Trump campaign bringing Steve Bannon of *Breibert* to serve as CEO of his campaign. In an impressive display of oppositional research, Clinton presented headlines from *Breitbart* stories that were shockingly sexist, racist, and just plain offensive, to demonstrate how Trump had embraced the fringe elements of alt-right extremist bigotry and reaction.[99]

The same day, Trump's labelling Clinton a "bigot" was replayed endlessly, and both candidates levelled charges of "racism" against each other. Not surprisingly, embarrassing stories began appearing about Trump's new campaign CEO *Brietbart News* hit man Steve Bannon. The *Guardian* reported "Trump campaign chief Steve Bannon is registered voter at vacant Florida home. Exclusive: Bannon's enrollment is apparent violation of crucial swing state's election law requiring voters to be legal residents of county they register in," and "Steve Bannon, Trump campaign CEO, faced domestic violence charges."[100] The Trump campaign had already had two of its campaign managers resign in disgrace, and pundits speculated how long the vile Bannon would hang in.

In another sign that his campaign was in disarray and that Trump was startlingly ignorant and confused, at a Town Hall meeting broadcast live on August 25 with Sean Hannity, the *Fox News* host who was Trump's most fanatic supporter, Trump asked the audience what his position should be on undocumented immigrant families who had lived in the U.S. for 15 years or more and were productive citizens. Trump asked the crowd whether they should "throw them out" or "work with them," in effect, providing a path to citizenship. Trump's "softening" of his stance on immigration created an uproar among his most fervent supporters who were virulently anti-immigrant, and Trump was forced to back-tract, showing that he did not even have a coherent position on his key issue and had no real policy on immigration (or anything else) at all!

During the weekend of August 27–28, Trump's surrogates appeared on the weekend news and talk shows insisting that Trump would not "soften" his stance on immigration and that the Trump Wall and Forced Deportation were still the key pillar of his candidacy – although pundits and surrogates speculated that Trump would modulate his position during his long-postponed "major speech" on immigration, supposedly forthcoming the coming week.

Trump surrogates were also being confronted with the proliferation of polls that were indicating that Trump had little chance of winning the election and that his poll numbers nationally and in key states showed no serious momentum, the Big Mo, that George H.W. Bush recognized was necessary to win a presidential election. Indeed, even in NASCAR country, the bastion of white working class male competitive sports that was supposed to be the strong foundation of Trump Country, there were reports that he was losing support.[101]

More telling, an increasing amount of Republican leaders were concluding that Trump was going to lose, and bring the Republican Party down with him, and were moving to distance themselves from him.[102] There was recognition that the $2 billion worth of free media that had helped him win the Republican primaries had a negative effect on many voters who formed a bad image of Trump as arrogant, racially and political divisive, and unfit to be president.[103]

Once again, Trump's mental health was becoming an issue when MSNBC's Mika Brzezinski stated that the time has come for a mental health professional to take a look at Donald Trump on "Morning Joe" show.[104] Brzezinski cited tweets sent by Trump over the weekend concerning the death of basketball star Dwyane Wade's cousin from gun violence in Chicago. Trump bragged how he had warned against growing violence in black communities in an incredibly insensitive tweet, gloating: "Dwayne [sic] Wade's cousin was just shot and killed walking her baby in Chicago. Just what I have been saying. African-Americans will VOTE TRUMP!" *The Guardian* noted: "A second, nearly identical tweet, with the spelling of Wade's name corrected, was sent soon after. Several hours later, Trump tweeted his condolences…It was not the first time that Trump's tweeted reaction to tragedy has drawn criticism. In the immediate aftermath of the June mass shooting in an Orlando, Florida, nightclub, Trump tweeted about people congratulating him for his foresight. 'Appreciate the congrats for being right on radical Islamic terrorism,'" he wrote. 'I don't want congrats, I want toughness & vigilance. We must be smart!'"[105]

These tweets reveal not only Trump's incredible insensitivity and lack of empathy, but full-blown out-of-control naracissism. For Trump, national tragedies involving violence prove that he was right, in these cases, that there is dangerous crime in African American communities and in Orlando that we face violence from radical Islamic terrorism. Every national tragedy is a chance for Trump to congratulate himself and solicit votes!

As the campaign morphed into its final weeks, it became de rigeur for celebrities and those with access to media to attack Trump. Magician Penn Gillette produced a widely seen video of a Donald Trump card trick where the guy can't do it right "because he's an idiot!" In a concert at the Staples Center in Los Angeles, Barbra Streisand had a magician on the stage who she claimed can read anyone's mind – "except Donald Trump's, because he doesn't have one." The August 28, 2016, episode of the surrealistic TV political satire *Braindead* featured the pregnant wife of a Senator complaining that every time Donald Trump came on television her baby started kicking her!

More seriously, questions were being asked concerning Donald Trump's lack of transparency concerning his failure to release his tax forms and the laughable medical record which he released that proclaimed the candidate's strength and stamina to be "extraordinary" and declared that he would be "the healthiest individual ever elected to the presidency." The doctor's letter was in poor English and when interviewers caught up with him, he looked like a shaggy dog who could have used a haircut several months before, laughed inappropriately, and was criticized by a litany of real doctors appearing on television raising questions about Trump's doctor's competency and the need for a real medical report, as Trump would be one of the oldest candidates to take office if he won.

As for Trump's taxes, every presidential candidate since the 1960s had released their tax forms which had become a standard practice in vetting candidates. With the publication of the *Trump Revealed. An American Journal of Ambition, Ego, Money, and Power* by Michael Kranish and Marc Fisher and a team of *Washington Post* reporters, new questions were raised about Trump's intricate empire of business dealings. Trump was involved in a myriad of deals with countless companies who bought Trump's name in partnerships in a variety of businesses, staggering bank loans to projects Trump and his organization were actually involved in, many of which failed, leaving partners and investors taking the loss, and deals with governments and shady characters throughout the world, all of whom could make claims on Trump were he to ascend to the presidency. It was also widely speculated that Trump was refusing to release his tax forms because he paid shockingly little in taxes because of his lifetime of scams and cons (and shocking tax breaks and abatements to real estate investors and the superrich). There were reports that Trump contributed much less to charity than he claimed, that he had much less money than he asserted because of his mountain of debt, and there were speculations that his tax forms might reveal that he had broken the law, or engaged in practices that would land him in scandal, if not jail.

On August 31, 2016, the day that Trump was scheduled to present his long-awaited speech on immigration, he announced a surprise trip to Mexico on his Twitter account. Once again, Trump dominated the cable news cycle as commentators speculated on his trip, showed his plane landing in Mexico, coming to Los Pinos, the Presidential residence, and meeting and then having a press conference with the Mexican President Enrique Peña Nieto, who had once compared

Trump to Mussolini and Hitler. At their joint press conference, both men spoke in diplomatic platitudes of the importance of Mexico for the United States and vice versa. Yet after the event, Trump claimed they had not discussed who would pay for the fabled wall that Trump promised to build along the Mexican border, while Peña Nieto claimed that he had told Trump that Mexico would not pay for the wall, though it was unlikely that he used the language of former Mexican President Vicente Fox who explained that Mexico "was not going to pay for the fucking wall."

Trump flew back to the U.S. to give his long-awaited immigration speech in Arizona, taking an extreme hard-line that there was "one route and one route only" for immigrants in the country illegally: "to return home and apply for re-entry like everybody else." He also insisted that "There will be no amnesty," and that he will carry out the deportations of more than two million immigrants, in "a matter of months," without detailing how this could happen. Yet his tone was unusually harsh and many thought that Trump had perhaps gone over the edge, leaving behind his more moderate followers.

Indeed, the next day there were reports that half of his Latino advisory committee had quit in disgust at Trump's hardline and failure to modulate his position as he had promised in discussions with them the previous weekend.[106] With the Republicans facing four more years in the wilderness, commentators speculated that historians may recall the raucous rally in Phoenix as a low point of the Trump campaign, perhaps even as the moment that he definitively extinguished his hopes of becoming president. That feeling will be particularly pronounced because it came at the end of a whirlwind media spectacle of a trip to Mexico that might otherwise have been remembered as a triumph.

The following day Trump's theme was patriotism and the flag, orating in Cincinnati that: "A Trump administration would consult with the military veterans' group to promote 'pride and patriotism' in schools – teaching respect" for the US flag and pledge of allegiance. "That flag deserves respect, and I will work with American Legion to help to strengthen respect for our flag," said Trump. "You see what's happening. It's very, very sad. And, by the way, we want young Americans to recite the pledge of allegiance. One country, under one constitution, saluting one American flag … always saluting." Reiterating the anti-immigration message at the heart of his campaign, Trump called to "advance the cause of Americanism – not globalism," and emphasized again his "America First" message: "We will be united by our common culture, values and principles – becoming one American nation."

Trump had been trolling for African American votes and planned a trip to Detroit over the Labor Day weekend to meet with African Americans and in anticipation of this great event, one of his surrogates, Pastor Mark Burns, released a Tweet with Hillary Clinton in blackface calling out: "Black Americans, THANK YOU FOR YOUR VOTES and letting me use you again… See you again in 4 years. pic.twitter. com/c4BOc6Tgkt—Pastor Mark Burns." In the cartoon, Clinton in blackface is depicted standing at a podium holding a sign reading, "#@!* the police" and "I ain't no ways tired of pandering to African-Americans."[107]

Although Burns apologized for the offensive video, the next day after vigorously defending it for one news cycle, commentators recalled that earlier Tweet Donald Trump himself had sent out an image of Hillary Clinton surrounded by stacks of money with a red star next to her face proclaiming "Most Corrupt Candidate ever!" – the star and image had been apparently taken from a white supremacist and anti-Semitic site deploying the Star of David.[108]

On the day before Trump's visit to Detroit, CNN was interviewing Mark Burn, who they confronted with false documents on his web-site and self-profile which claimed he had a Bachelor of Science degree and served six years in the Army Reserve. When CNN got Burns to admit that he was never in the Army Reserve and never received a Bachelor's degree, he responded with Trumpian anger, and then said that the false information on his website had "obviously" been either "manipulated or either hacked or added" – although the site host, Wix, confirmed that there was no evidence of a hack, revealing another major Trump surrogate as a liar and con, following the steps of the Master Con and Liar of all, Donald J. Trump.

Indeed, the *New York Times* revealed that Trump's planned meeting with African Americans in Detroit was scripted, releasing an eight-page script of questions and answers that were determined in advanced of Trump's ballyhooed "dialogue" with African Americans.[109] Trump's meeting with African Americans in a church building in Philadelphia before his Detroit visit was also revealed as a fraud, as the meeting was packed with hand-picked black people sitting around the table with Trump, while the Pastor Herb Lusk was on vacation in Mexico. When Pastor Lusk found out what happened in his church, he said that he had not authorized it, and that "it was probably a business arrangement" (i.e Trump's people rented the space and paid token blacks to show up).[110]

Reports had circulated without too much media attention that veteran operative David Bossie had joined the Trump cabal as deputy campaign manager. Rachel Maddow opened her September 3, 2016 *The Rachel Maddow Show* with a long report indicating that Bossie had been one of the original Dirty Tricksters sent by the Republican Right back in the 1990s to dig up dirt on the Clintons, and that his tactics and smears were so bad that then President George H.W. Bush referred to him as "one of the lowest forms of life" and distanced his campaign from Bossie's dirty tricks and slander. David Bossie was a propaganda and slur specialist who had devoted a life-time to attacking the Clintons, coming out with a 2008 documentary *Hillary the Movie*. Bossie gained national renown and infamy in 2010 when as President of a rightwing lobby-group Citizens United, his group successfully won a Supreme Court case that overturned restrictions on campaign-finance reform and opened the door for secret megadollars to be deployed in political campaigns – a decision that both Bernie Sanders and Hillary Clinton had vowed to overturn.[111]

So now one of the sleaziest rightwing operatives in the country was working with Roger Ailes and Steven Bannon as part of the Trump Hillary Clinton attack squad and it was just a question of how far would they go. Trump had a coalition at the top of his campaign of the most unprincipled ideologues and operatives of the far right, and had brought extremism and the alt-right into the heart of U.S. politics, reconstructing his campaign into a cabal of hate.

FROM LABOR DAY WEEK TO NOVEMBER 6:
THE FINAL BATTLE

Conventional wisdom holds that the Fall U.S. presidential campaigns begin in earnest after the Labor Day weekend, and that people aren't really focusing on the election until the final weeks. It is doubtful that this is true in the Clinton-Trump slugfest, since Trump's campaign has gone on full steam for almost 18 months, while Hillary Clinton has been running for president for decades. While Trump totally dominated the news cycles during the last two weeks in August, Clinton went on fund-raising tours in California, the Hamptons, and other Meccas of liberal wealth, putting together a formidable war chest to counter any attacks from TrumpWorld.

While in early August, Clinton had been around 8 points ahead in most polls, by Labor Day, Trump had pulled even in many major polls and even ahead in one. Hence, anything could happen in the next two months, although focus intensified on the presidential debates that were often crucial in determining who would win the election. The Labor Day weekend talk shows dissected Trump's attempt to reach out to African American voters and if it would have much effect, and Hillary Clinton's continual epic trouble with her "damned email," to use Bernie Sanders' evocative phrase. Both Clinton and Trump had the highest negatives of major party presidential candidates in history,[112] and much of both of their campaigns had focused on attacking the other candidate as both a danger to the U.S., and as completely unfit to serve as president.

On Labor Day, Donald Trump and Hillary Clinton made competing pitches in Ohio, setting the stage for a critical month in their testy and increasingly close presidential campaigns. Trump seemed to equivocate on his position on immigration and said that his major focus henceforth would be on "jobs." Yet with a military security forum coming up on September 7, both candidates began focusing on military security with Trump intoning in Philadelphia that he wants to talk about "three crucial words – Peace through strength." Yet this phrase is not a policy, but is a banal talking point, and Trump had yet to reveal his much-touted "secret plan" to destroy ISIS, nor had he laid out his plans for the military, beyond claiming that he would make the U.S. military the greatest in the world. Clinton portrayed Trump as a bungling businessman, unequipped to serve as commander in chief. and mockingly stated: "He [Trump] says he has a secret plan to defeat ISIS. The secret is, he has no plan." Clinton repeatedly trumpeted her vast experiences as the nation's top diplomat and her long experience in government, while her running mate, Senator Tim Kaine of Virginia in his first national security address, spelled out a contrast between Secretary Clinton's extensive experience and competency and Trump's lack of government experience and unfitness to serve as president.

For weeks, the Clinton campaign had been denounced for the Clinton Foundation taking donations from people with whom Hillary Clinton had met during her tenure as Secretary of State, and Trump repeatedly denounced her "pay-to-play politics," making it a major media theme. Yet charges surfaced that Trump donated $25,000 to a group supporting the Florida attorney general, Pam Bondi, perhaps to sway her office's review of fraud allegations at Trump University. Indeed, Trump's check arrived four days before Bondi ruled that Florida was not going to join the suit against Trump University, making it appear that Trump was involved in "pay-to-play," something that he had previously bragged that he excelled at as a businessman. Further, it was revealed that Trump's contribution to Bondi was not reported to the Internal Revenue Service (IRS), and he had been forced to pay a $2,500 penalty to the IRS, which was seen as "only the latest slap of his wrist in a decades-long record of shattering political donation limits and circumventing the rules governing contributions and lobbying."[113]

At the NBC-sponsored Commander-in-Chief Forum on military security staged on the Intrepid Sea, Air & Space Museum in Manhattan on September 7, 2016, Trump followed Clinton with each candidate getting thirty minutes to answer questions from the NBC anchor Matt Lauer and military veterans who were in the audience.[114] Clinton was put on the defensive with questions about her use of private e-mail servers, her vote for the Iraq war, her alleged hawkishness, and record as Secretary of State, while Trump was questioned about a crass Twitter message from 2013 in which he suggested that sexual assaults in the military were a logical result of men and women serving together. Refusing to back down, Trump answered: "It is a correct tweet."

When Lauer asked if Trump actually believed he knew more about ISIS than American generals, the candidate replied: "The generals have been reduced to rubble." Trump falsely claimed he had opposed the Iraq war from the beginning when there were widely circulated tapes of an interview with Howard Stern where Trump asserted he supported the Iraq war as it unfolded, and he repeated his wild assertion that the U.S. should have invaded Iraq and seized its oil. Breaking with precedent, Trump claimed that during his top-secret briefing with U.S. intelligence he could tell by their body language that the intelligence establishment was "not happy" because "our leaders did not follow what they were recommending." Further, he claimed that President Obama and Secretary Clinton, had done "exactly the opposite" of what the intelligence community recommended.

After the Forum, intelligence professionals insisted that their briefers were highly professional, did not reveal their political views through "body language," and that the briefers never revealed any divergence from the sitting administration. Further, experts claimed that candidates who were given intelligence reports in top-secret briefings were not supposed to discuss the event with the public, and that Trump's comments were completely inappropriate.[115]

When Matt Lauer brought up Trump's admiration for Russian President Vladimir Putin at the Forum, noting that Mr. Putin had invaded Ukraine, was occupying Crimea, and was suspected of hacking Democratic emails, Trump refused to say a negative word about him, answering: "Do you want me to start naming some of the things that President Obama does?" – a revealing statement that questions Trump's judgment and his inexplicable refusal to criticize Putin.

Indeed, Trump repeatedly insisted that Putin was a stronger leader for Russia than Obama was for the U.S., making it crystal clear that Trump's political ideal was strongmen, authoritarian leaders who disregarded international law, human rights, and democracy, while championing aggression, extreme nationalism, and militarism, exactly Trump's position. Indeed, Trump himself, as I have argued, *is* an authoritarian, in his disposition, his contempt for the judiciary, media, and other division of powers, and his militarism and aggressiveness exhibited in his foreign policy promises to "bomb the shit out of ISIS," bring back torture "and worse," and to be "the most militarist" candidate who will "make America great again."

Yet, with the uproar over the Commander-in-Chief Forum, the media neglected to dissect the incredible speech that Trump had given in Philadelphia just before the Forum where he advocated an astonishing build-up for the military. In an invitation-only event in the Union League of Philadelphia, Trump called for hundreds more new U.S. ships, planes and submarines, and a "state of the art" missile defense system. He would begin with modernizing 22 Navy cruisers at a cost of about $220 million apiece, and would raise U.S. troop levels to 540,000, vowing to train thousands more combat troops. Echoing Ronald Reagan in calling for "peace through strength." Trump, in effect, was projecting the largest military expansion in U.S. history.

The following day commentators buzzed about Trump's love affair with Putin and seeming aversion to criticizing a man who Trump claimed had called him "brilliant," repeating his standard line that when "someone says something nice about me, I say something nice about them," leading pundits to note that all a foreign leader needs to do is to praise Trump and they can play him as a sucker. There was also research by NBC, laid out in full on *The Rachel Maddow Show* on September 8, 2016, that Putin had not really called Trump "brilliant," but used a Russian word better translated as "bright-shining," "flamboyant," or "colorful" to describe him. Other foreign policy experts on cable television were appalled by Trump's lack of foreign policy knowledge, his bromance with Putin, and his insults of the U.S. president and top military leaders.

On September 9, 2016, Trump appeared on Kremlin-funded channel RT (previously called "Russia Today") for a call-in interview with his old buddy Larry King, who had chosen a strange venue for his swan-song to a long life of doing softball interviews. After a media uproar, the Trump campaign claimed that Trump didn't know what channel he was on in the interview, with his hapless campaign manager Kelly Anne Conway tweeting just before dawn's early light:

> He…did an intw w Larry King, a personal friend of his… He didn't know it would be on Russian TV. @kellyannepolls on Trump's intw on RT

4:34 AM–9 Sep 2016[116]

Trump took the occasion to attack U.S. foreign policy, media, and the political system. When asked by King if he believed, as had been widely reported, that Russia had hacked the DNC, perhaps to help Trump, Trump reiterated that he didn't believe that the Russians had done the hack, putting him at odds again with U.S. intelligence agencies, and raising the question of what intelligence sources Trump avails himself of.[117]

Throughout the campaign, Trump has viciously attacked Barack Obama and linked Clinton with Obama's presidency that Trump describes as "failed," the "worst ever," and still worse. At the final press conference Obama held at the Association of Southeast Asian Nations' summit in Laos on September 8, Obama broke into a laugh when asked to respond to Donald Trump's remark that Vladimir Putin was "a leader, far more than our President has been a leader." Asked if he wanted to "defend" his legacy from Trump's criticism, Obama smiled and answered: "Do I care to defend…? OK, OK, respond," he said, laughing. "As far as Mr. Trump, I think I've already offered my opinion," Obama said. "I don't think the guy's qualified to be president of the United States. Every time he speaks that opinion is confirmed."

Becoming serious, Obama warned that Trump's "unacceptable and outrageous" behavior is becoming normalized in the 2016 election cycle, and stated a concern that Trump's behavior was not being scrutinized closely enough by the press who he suggested should take another look at Trump's "outright whacky ideas," and hoped that the American public will examine Trump's track record "and make a good decision."

After several days in which media focus had been levelled at Trump for his outrageous comments at the Commander-in-Chief Forum, attention turned to Hillary Clinton when at a private fundraiser with Barbra Streisand on September 9, she claimed that half of Trump's followers belonged in "a basket of deplorables," which she described as consisting of "the racist, sexist, homophobic, xenophobic, Islamaphobic – you name it." She went on to note "some of those folks – they are irredeemable, but thankfully they are not America".

The Trump campaign picked up on the "basket of deplorables," using it to portray Clinton as showing contempt for Trump supporters. Clinton immediately partially retracted her statement, saying that while it was clearly wrong to put half of Trump's supporters in a basket, some of his supporters surely exhibited deplorable tendencies like racism, sexism, homophobia, xenophobia, and other bad tendencies. Clinton, then, refocused her attack, saying that Trump had "built his campaign largely on prejudice and paranoia and given a national platform to hateful views and voices". She also conceded: "Many of Trump's supporters are hard-working Americans who just don't feel like the economy or our political system are working for them."

HILLARY'S STUMBLE, TRANSPARENCY, AND HEALTH/TAXES

On Sunday September 11, 2016, media attention shifted as both Hillary Clinton and Donald Trump suspended campaigning to mark the 15th anniversary of the 9/11 attacks in a ceremony at Ground Zero, making a rare joint appearance to denote unity in the face of terrorism. While the Sunday morning talk shows were debating whether Clinton's characterizing Trump supporters as a "basket of deplorables" would harm her campaign, suddenly there were "Breaking News" reports that Hillary Clinton had abruptly left a ceremony in New York honoring the 15th anniversary of the September 11 attacks, and had to be helped into a van by Secret Service agents. Soon there appeared I-phone images, that would be repeated for days to come, of Clinton being assisted, and then stumbling and falling into the van.

Next, breaking into regularly scheduled programs, the media reported that Clinton was resting in the Manhattan apartment of her daughter, Chelsea, and around 90 minutes from her arrival, there was another "Breaking News" segment showing Clinton emerging from Chelsea's apartment and waving with a smile to onlookers. Clinton stopped to talk and pose for pictures with a little girl, and answering reporters asking how she was doing, and smiling she responded: "I'm feeling great. It's a beautiful day in New York." She got into a car and left, and reporters soon after indicated that she had returned to her Chappaqua, N.Y. residence sometime after 1 p.m., and Clinton was not seen publicly the rest of the day.

Initially, the Clinton campaign released a report saying that the candidate was feeling "overheated," and became "dehydrated" at the 9/11 ceremony, and then around 5 p.m a campaign official announced that Mrs. Clinton's physician, Dr. Lisa R. Bardack, had examined the candidate at her home in Chappaqua, and stated that Clinton was "rehydrated and recovering nicely." Further, the statement indicated that: "Secretary Clinton has been experiencing a cough related to allergies," adding that on Friday morning, after a prolonged cough, Mrs. Clinton was diagnosed with pneumonia and was being treated with antibiotics. The next day, Clinton cancelled a California fund-raising trip.

For once, Trump remained quiet and the next day released a get-well wish "so she could get back on the campaign trail," but qualified his statement by immediately saying "I don't know what's going on," and then a few sentences later proclaimed "Something's going on," which is his conspiracy code word, signaling to his followers that a conspiracy is going on. In any case, the spectacle of Hillary's Stumble, which had occurred after months of questions about her health from Trump and his surrogates, raised the issue of the health of the two oldest candidates to run for the presidency, and increased pressure on both Clinton and Trump to release detailed medical records.

Indeed, *transparency* was emerging as a key campaign theme. Neither Trump nor Clinton had satisfied demands that they be transparent in terms of health and tax records and access to media. Trump had released what serious physicians saw as a bogus medical report and obviously there would be new demands for Clinton's medical records. Clinton had released tax records, as had every presidential candidate since Richard Nixon in the 1960s, but Trump had yet to do so, making the bogus claim that he was being audited – an activity that had not prevented previous presidential candidates from releasing their tax returns. As noted earlier, there were serious questions concerning Trump's business deals, debts, who he was obligated to, how much in taxes he has payed, and whether he is really as wealthy as he has claimed.

September 12 was dominated by speculation concerning Clinton's health and previous health issues of various candidates and presidents. Both candidates promised to release full health records later in the week and Clinton's surrogates, including Bill Clinton, went on TV to proclaim how healthy Hillary was while the networks played over and over the montage of "Hillary's Stumble" which had become one of the major political spectacles of the campaign and perhaps of recent U.S. presidential history. When Bill Clinton inadvertently said "this has happened to Hillary before," again there was a rash of speculation concerning deeper medical problems, leading Hillary to call Anderson Cooper on CNN during his evening show and assuring him that she was resting and well, while Cooper grilled Clinton relentlessly about her health.

During the day, the nation was treated to past TV montage of President Gerald Ford stumbling and slipping while go up the stairs of the presidential jet, George H.W. Bush throwing up on a Japanese official during a state dinner in Japan, George Jr. telling how he'd choked on a pretzel while watching football and called the White House nurse to help him dislodge the pesky pretzel. And there were reports about how previous presidents had not revealed major diseases including FDR who suffered polio, forcing him to travel in a wheelchair, JFK who suffered Addison's disease that forced him to wear tight and painful back braces, and Ike who'd had heart attacks in office. Finally, *The Rachel Maddow Show* provided a montage of numerous younger and older people fainting at presidential rallies in the recent past, evidently demonstrating how common it was to faint and stumble at U.S. political events.

Meanwhile, Trump kept up his relentless hammering at Clinton's alleged assault on his supporters with her "basket of deplorables" label, and cable network panels debated who Trump's deplorables were and how many there were. At a Trump rally in Asheville, North Carolina multiple physical confrontations between Trump supporters and security staff and non-Trump supporters erupted, with images of a Trump supporter punching a protestor, while another video caught Trump security guy Eddie Deck confronting a protestor and threatening: "You're going to go, too, in 2 fucking seconds" (see https://t.co/iZ1Y5Z2pb6). And trumpeting his unrestrained militarist tendencies on a National Public Radico (NPR) interview, Trump said that if Iran harasses U.S. ships in the Persian Gulf, "they will be shot out of the water," leading military experts to denounced Trump's reckless blustering.[118]

Hillary Clinton announced that she would return to the campaign trail on Thursday, and both she and Donald Trump indicated that they would both release more detailed medical records, setting off a storm of discussion concerning medical issues and transparency for two of the oldest candidates to run for president. Trump's earlier released medical statement was taken to be a joke (see above, pp. 73–74), and he continued the reality TV show mode of campaigning by announcing that he would release his medical records to TV-Dr. Oz on his medical show who would question him, setting up a media spectacle where Donald Trump would make his alleged medical records literally part of a reality TV show.

Meanwhile, on September 13, Barack Obama made his first solo campaign appearance this election cycle in a dynamic speech in Philadelphia, broadcast live on the cable networks and proving that Obama was still the best campaigner and speech-maker in the U.S. political system. Obama defended his record and positive achievements,[119] while attacking Donald Trump for fanning the flames of "anger and hate," and offering "a dark, pessimistic vision of a country where we turn against each other, we turn away from the rest of the world."

Obama voiced his frustration with how the election was being covered, complaining about media reports for creating "a false equivalency" between the two nominees. Obama noted how there had been focus on both Clinton Foundation and Trump Foundation alleged scandals in recent weeks, but Obama argued that: "One candidate's family foundation has saved countless lives around the world." Yet "the other candidate's foundation [i.e. Trump's] took money other people gave to his charity and then bought a six-foot-tall painting of himself. He had the taste not to go for the 10-foot version." The tacky picture of Donald Trump that Obama spoke of provided 30 seconds of fame for the artist and viral reproduction of the picture.

Obama complained that Trump's daily controversies and scandals has meant that "our standard for what's normal has changed," and "You don't grade the presidency on a curve." If "you want to debate transparency," Obama noted, "you have one candidate in this debate who's released decades worth of her tax returns. The other candidate is the first in decades who refuses to release any at all." Bringing his ringing endorsement to a close, Obama asserted that those who believed in his agenda should vote for Clinton in November, repeating his DNC claim that Clinton was the most qualified individual to ever aspire to the presidency, while Trump "isn't fit in any shape or form" to serve as commander-in-chief.

The same day reports circulated that former secretary of defense and retired four-star general Colin Powell's email had been hacked, and in one email he referred to Donald Trump as a "national disgrace" and an "international pariah." In an another email Powell noted that Trump's promotion of the "birther" myth Obama was "racist," while in an email to former secretary of state Condoleezza Rice, Powell called the Benghazi affair a "stupid witch hunt," and Rice replied: "Completely agree." Powell, however, had negative things to say as well about Hillary and Bill Clinton and noted that "I would rather not have to vote for [her]."[120]

There were allegations that the Powell hack, like the DNC hack, had been by the Russians who were allegedly trying to interfere with, or delegitimize, the U.S. presidential election. Republican Congressman Rep. Michael McCaul (R-Texas), chairman of the House Homeland Security Committee, appeared on CNN and claimed that the Republican National Committee (RNC) was also hacked, although material had not yet been released. Yet the RNC had previously denied this, and the Congressman dialed back his claim after his appearance, saying that "some" Republicans had been hacked. The question of interference and the possibility of an "October Surprise" that could reveal material that could sway the election was worrisome, as was the response of Trump supporters, who if they lost a close election might call the election rigged and erupt violently. Indeed, one prominent Trump supporter, Kentucky Governor Matt Bevin, predicted that there would be a "shedding of the blood of tyrants and patriots" if Clinton were to be named president in November.[121]

Newsweek published an explosive story by Kurt Eichenwald, "How the Trump organization's foreign business ties could upend U.S. national security,"[122] which documented that the Trump Organization is a global octopus "with deep ties to global financiers, foreign politicians and even criminals, although there is no evidence the Trump Organization has engaged in any illegal activities." Eichenwald raised questions whether if Trump is elected president, would he and his family permanently sever all connections to the Trump Organization, "a sprawling business empire that has spread a secretive financial web across the world? Or will Trump instead choose to be the most conflicted president in American history, one whose business interests will constantly jeopardize the security of the United States?"

MSNBC's *The Rachel Maddow Show* played clips of Trump saying that he would not be active in the Trump organization were he to become president, and that his children would run the organization, which, of course, begs the question of whether Trump would act as president to help his secretive financial empire, or whether elements of it could coerce Trump into acting against U.S. interests. Previously, presidential candidates had put their business interests in a blind trust, but Trump had not provided a serious answer concerning what he would do with his business interests after the election were he to win, and few reporters had queried him on the issue.

Trump had another embarrassing episode on September 14, when he landed in Flint, Michigan to inspect their water crisis. Flint Mayor Karen Weaver was in Washington lobbying Congress for federal help, and expressed unhappiness with the trip, saying she was unaware of his plans to visit, and that neither Trump nor his staff had reached out since the crisis was declared an emergency. "Flint is focused on fixing the problems caused by lead contamination of our drinking water, not photo ops," Weaver noted. After examining the new water purification system and replacement of pipes, far from completed, Trump bragged how he could fix it quick. During remarks at a Methodist church soon afterward, he started attacking Hillary Clinton and her "failed" policies – and was promptly chastised when the Pastor ran up to the podium and said: "Mr. Trump, I invited you here to thank us for what we've done in Flint. Not to give a political speech." Trump looked surprised, said "OK," and quickly wound up his appearance in the black church. Later, he called the Pastor a "nervous mess," unable to stop himself from attacking anyone who angers him in any way.[123]

At another stop that day in Canton Ohio, Trump publicly raised questions about Hillary Clinton's health for the first time since Secretary Clinton had left the campaign trail on Sunday to recover from peunomia. Speaking in an air-conditioned minor league basketball arena Trump mocked Clinton, saying: "You think this is easy? In this beautiful room that's 122 degrees. It is hot, and it is always hot when I perform because the crowds are so big. The rooms were not designed for this kind of crowd. I don't know, folks. You think Hillary Clinton would be able to stand up here and do this for an hour? I don't know."

Earlier, Trump had taped his appearance on "The Dr. Oz Show" which was to be aired the next day. Trump had previously said that he would release findings of his most recent examination by his long-time Doctor Harold Bornstein on the show, but then his campaign said that he was not releasing the results. Playing in a tease mode, Trump asked the audience if they wanted to see the results of his recent exam and when they shouted in the affirmative, Trump handed Dr. Oz a sheet of paper listing the results of the physical with the discredited Doctor.

Trump also provided to *The Washington Post* a document that summarizes his latest physical exam, saying he takes a cholesterol-lowering drug and is overweight but overall is in "excellent physical health." Fat Donald weighed in at 236 pounds and 6'3" tall, making him overweight for his height. His "laboratory results" from a blood test and other exams were also given, indicating that:

> he has a cholesterol level of 169, with his level of high-density lipoproteins at 63, his low-density lipoproteins at 94.

> The businessman's blood pressure is 116 over 70. His blood sugar level is 99 milligrams per deciliter. Trump's level of triglycerides, which are a type of fat in blood, is 61 milligrams per deciliter. And his prostate-specific antigen level is measured as 0.15. His liver function and thyroid function tests are all within the normal range, Bornstein writes, adding that "his last colonoscopy was performed on July 10, 2013 which was normal and revealed no polyps".

> Trump's latest electrocardiogram test and chest X-ray took place in April 2016 and were "normal."

> With regard to Trump's heart, Bornstein writes that "his cardiac evaluation included a transthoracic echocardiogram"

in December 2014 and "this study was reported within the range of normal."

Bornstein notes that there is "no family history of premature cardiac or neoplastic disease" and that Trump's parents, Fred and Mary, "lived into their late 80s and 90s."

Trump's testosterone level is 441.6.

"I feel as good today as I did when I was 30," Trump said on the show, according to another clip.[124]

Doctors on cable news shows insisted that Trump's health record wasn't as transparent as it seemed, that Dr. Bornstein's rushed examination was problematic, and that Dr. Oz had been in trouble with charges of his hawking fraudulent products and cures, and that Trump was exploiting the serious issue of presidential health by participating in a media spectacle on a TV reality show.

Trump had his children out as surrogates and they weren't having a good day. Donald Jr told a Philadelphia radio station that "the media has been [Hillary Clinton's] number one surrogate in this," and "without the media, this wouldn't even be a contest, but the media has built her up. They've let her slide on every indiscrepancy [sic], on every lie, on every DNC game trying to get Bernie Sanders out of this thing. If Republicans were doing that, they'd be warming up the gas chamber right now."

Spokespeople for Jewish groups, the Clinton campaign, and many pundits said that Donald Jr. went over the line of decency by exploiting the Holocaust to make a (dicey) political point. Ivanka too had a bad day, breaking off an interview with *Cosmopolitan* over her father's freshly released child-care and maternity-leave plan. The night before in the break-out of the Trump child-care initiative, Ivanka, standing next to her father, claimed that "little intellectual energy" had gone into child-care policy and the Clinton team had not offered one. The *Cosmo* interviewer, however, pointed out that: "Hillary Clinton released [aspects of] her plan over a year ago. Why did the Trump campaign wait so long to release this policy?" Ivanka also had no answer as to why no paternity leave was included in the plan, why gay men were excluded, and when the interviewer brought up a 2004 comment that Donald Trump made about pregnancy being inconvenient for business, Ivanka had had enough, indignantly replying before she broke off the interview and left:

> So I think that you have a lot of negativity in these questions, and I think my father has put forth a very comprehensive and really revolutionary plan to deal with a lot of issues. So I don't know how useful it is to spend too much time with you on this if you're going to make a comment like that. My father obviously has a track record of decades of employing women at every level of his company, and supporting women, and supporting them in their professional capacity, and enabling them to thrive outside of the office and within. To imply otherwise is an unfair characterization of his track record and his support of professional women.[125]

On September 16, 2016, on one of the most deplorable days in a deplorable campaign Trump said in an interview on *Fox Business* that he would make "a big announcement" about his stance on the president's birthplace during a campaign event at his new downtown Washington luxury hotel. The press speculated that finally Trump himself would address the birther issue, for during the past weeks, Trump's campaign spokespeople assured interviewers that they believed Barack Obama was born in the USA and so did Donald Trump. Yet Trump steadfastly refused to end the controversy with a simple statement. When during an interview with *The Washington Post*, Trump refused to comment on the birther issue, but suggested he would later,[126] there was feverish media discussions of Trump and the birther controversy, and speculation as to whether he'd finally admit that Obama was indeed born in the U.S.

Assembling the press corps in his new hotel was a good publicity stunt, and on the stage in a press reception room, Trump surrounded himself with veterans, who one after another praised Trump. The cable news networks were broadcasting the great event live, and finally the CNN crew broke off coverage, angry that Trump had promised an important announcement and turned it into a campaign event and more free TV for the Donald. Cutting off the peeved cable commentariat, suddenly Deplorable Donald strode up to the microphone and stated that:

> Hillary Clinton and her campaign of 2008 started the birther controversy. I finished it. I finished it. You know what I mean. President Barack Obama was born in the United States, period. Now we all want to go back to making America strong again.

Although Trump had claimed that his "big announcement" would be part of a press conference, he walked out of the hotel with the frustrated media shouting questions at him, and angry reporters tweeting that they'd been duped again by Trump, that it was a lie that Hillary Clinton had "started the birther" controversy, and it would certainly not be Donald Trump who ended it, as Trump had again made the birther issue a burning theme in the campaign that went to the heart of concerns about Deplorable Donald's qualifications and fitness to be president. Throughout the event, the *Guardian* was publishing tweets critical of Trump's deceptive manipulation of the press,[127] and he was bombarded with questions and negative tweets as he left the fake press conference.

The *Washington Post* accurately headlined its' story covering the (pseudo)event "Trump admits Obama was born in U.S., but falsely blames Clinton for starting rumors."[128] Shortly after Trump's pseudo media event, members of the Black Congressional Caucus emerged in a state of rage for a press conference to denounce Trump. One after another, major leaders of Caucus strode up to the microphone and denounced Trump as a con, fraud, liar, and bully, and promised to mobilize voters of color and white voters to defeat Deplorable Donald in the November election. Indeed, Trump's denial that he was the father of the birther movement was a Big Lie and blaming the birther myth on Hillary Clinton was a Brazen Lie. Commentators and journalists dutifully assembled quotes over a five-year period documenting that Deplorable Donald had indeed fostered, promoted, and defended that myth that Barack Obama had not been born in the United States.[129]

Lying was the essence of Donald Trump, he told lie after lie, day after day, effortlessly, shamelessly, and boldly, but perhaps never had he told a bigger lie than his denial that he was the Godfather of Birtherism, nor had he told a more brazen lie than pinning the controversy on Clinton. In a press conference, Hillary Clinton pointed out that Trump's campaign was rooted in Birtherism, that he had promoted the myth for five years, and owed President Obama and the American people an explanation. Indeed, it was Donald Trump's promotion of the birther myth that first attracted attention for him on the far right and then in the Tea Party movement that emerged in 2010 to attack both mainstream Democratic and Republican policies, especially over immigration, an issue that Trump owned.

Trump had successfully stoked and mobilized the hatred of Barack Obama evident in far right groups and the Tea Party and others who could not stand having a black president, and whom hated everything about Barack Obama, believing him to be African-born, a Muslim, and a mysterious man without a past, all myths that Trump had stoked over the years. These same groups hated immigrants, foreigners, people of color, and those who they saw as "other," and Trump played on their anger and fears, presenting himself as the one candidate that would take up their causes, stand up to the "establishment," reverse the course of American politics, and "Make America Great Again" – for conservative white men and women who shared their grievances and anger.

Consequently, Trump had avoided renouncing birtherism because it was an essential pillar of the belief system of his most fervent supporters and perhaps he had even persuaded himself to believe it. Yet he had fallen behind in the polls and his new election team evidently were pushing him to appeal to white suburban women and more affluent Republican voters who did not buy into birthism; it would also make it easier for black Republicans to vote for Trump. Yet Trump's long overdue denial of the myth had outraged blacks, gained a lot of negative media attention just when Trump was rising again in the polls, and was framed by a deplorable lie that Hillary Clinton had started the controversy and, he, Trump had ended it.

By the afternoon, Trump was back to outrageous lies and provocations, telling a group of gun rights advocates at a Miami rally that Hillary Clinton was "against the Second Amendment" and was going to take their guns away. Trump opened his event with the unfurling of a new "Les Deplorables" battlefield flag backdrop, and becoming unhinged, Trump called for Clinton's bodyguards to "disarm immediately" – adding, "Let's see what happens to her." Hinting at a call for her assassination, the ploy followed up an earlier call for "Second Amendment" people to "do something" if Trump was denied the election, which had been interpreted as an incitement to shoot Hillary Clinton if Trump was not elected. Clinton's campaign manager Robby Mook quickly responded and denounced Trump's comments: "Donald Trump, the Republican nominee for President, has a pattern of inciting people to violence. Whether this is done to provoke protesters at a rally or casually or even as a joke, it is an unacceptable quality in anyone seeking the job of Commander in Chief."[130]

Yet polls were beginning to show Donald Trump pulling ahead. In a September 14, 2016 story in *The Washington Post*, Chris Cillizza warned: "Don't look now: Donald Trump has all the momentum in the 2016 race."[131] Cillizza writes that "Trump has seized the momentum from Hillary Clinton and is climbing back into contention in both national and key swing state polling," gaining the lead in significant swing states and pulling within just four points in some national polls, whereas Clinton had been leading in double digits in many polls following the Democratic National convention.

The first presidential debate on September 27, 2016, was the ultimate political media spectacle. From the outset, Trump played to the hilt the authoritarian macho shouting, insulting Clinton, and trying to dominate the procedure; Clinton, however, ignored Trump's bullying and blustering, made her arguments against him, and presented her positions on the issues. As the debate progressed, Trump exhibited a loss of stamina, rambled, became incoherent, and suffered Clinton sharply attacking his business record, his failure to pay taxes, his atrocious attacks on women, and his lack of qualifications to be president. Trump's unraveling during the debate presented the media spectacle of the Outsider and Macho Man, not ready for prime time and losing the debate to the cool professional and qualified politician, who was able to provide coherent answers to questions, attack and put in place her opponent and generally dominate the debate spectacle.

The next morning after what commentators on all sides labeled a disappointing, and even disastrous, debate, Trump went on the attack, lashing out at the debate moderator, complaining about his microphone and threatening to make Bill Clinton's marital infidelity a campaign issue in a spectacle of desperation. There were estimates that 85 million people had watched the debate live on television and millions more were rewatching it and discussing it at home, work, and online, making it one of the major spectacles in US political history. Clinton was exuberant, campaigning with Bernie Sanders presenting a united Democratic Party on the offensive.

Presidential debates are the ultimate shared media spectacle and it would be interesting to see if Trump could recover and gain the offensive in the coming political debates and last weeks of the campaign. At different stages, Clinton and Trump had dominated the presidential spectacle, and anything could happen, as was shown when the video tape surfaced on October 7 with Donald Trump's extremely lewd remarks towards women.[132]

The 2016 U.S. presidential election was turning out to be one of the most dramatic, hotly contested, and consequential in history. It was a media spectacle that engrossed much of the country and the world, although many found the campaign to be deplorable and were deeply dissatisfied with both candidates. This study has focused on Donald Trump and the Trump phenomenon which is unprecedented in U.S. history and which I focus on in the provisionally concluding remarks.

TO BE CONTINUED...

PROVISIONAL CONCLUSION

Reading a stack of books and countless articles on Trump and following his life closely since he has announced for presidency, I see Donald J. Trump as a paragon of what Herbert Marcuse called "one-dimensional man."[133] Trump's one-dimension is his gigantic ego that must be fed with unlimited amounts of adulation, money, power, and attention. His ego extends to his family that no doubt he sees as extensions of himself or part of his business enterprise (which they literally are). Trump seems to have no life-long friends, no interests or hobbies beyond his business and now political enterprise, no interest in culture or ideas, beyond those he can exploit in his business or political campaign, and, as, biographers have noted, he does not seemed to be burdened with selfhood that involves depth, self-reflection, or self-awareness, let alone self-criticism, beyond an overwhelming sense of self-importance.

Trump has a gloomy pessimistic view of the world encapsulated in the philosophical vision that: "Man is the most vicious of all animals, and life is a series of battles ending in victory or defeat. You just can't let people make a sucker out of you."[134] Winning is all for one-dimensional Trump, the only purpose of life, the only thing worth pursuing, and the organizing principle of the Donald's existence. To win, Trump will do anything, raising the specter of what would a losing Trump do with nuclear weapons under his control, and what destruction might his unrestrained Ego and uncontrollable Id unleash upon the world if Trump is threatened in any sort of way. It is also worrisome to contemplate that Trump has developed a large following through his demagoguery and that authoritarian populism constitutes an American Nightmare, and a clear and present danger to US democracy and global peace and stability.

NOTES

1   On my concept of media spectacle, see Douglas Kellner, *Grand Theft 2000. Media Spectacle and a Stolen Election.* Lanham, Md.: Rowman and Littlefield, 2001; *Media Spectacle.* London and New York: Routledge, 2003; *From September 11 to Terror War: The Dangers of the Bush Legacy.* Lanham, Md.: Rowman and Littlefield, 2003; *Media Spectacle and the Crisis of Democracy.* Boulder, Col.: Paradigm Press, 2005; and *Media Spectacle and Insurrection, 2011: From the Arab Uprisings to Occupy Everywhere.* London and New York: Continuum/Bloomsbury, 2012.

2   I provide accounts of the O.J. Simpson Trial and the Clinton sex/impeachment scandal in the mid-1990s in M*edia Spectacle*, op. cit.; I engage the stolen election of 2000 in the Bush/Gore presidential campaign in *Grand Theft 2000*, op. cit., and describe the 9/11 terrorist attacks and their aftermath in *From 9/11 to Terror War*, op. cit.

3   See Kellner, *Media Spectacle and Insurrection,* 2011.

4   See Michael D'Antonio, *Never Enough. Donald Trump and the Pursuit of Success* (New York: Thomas Dunne Books, 2015); Gwenda Blair, *The Trumps* (New York: Simon and Schuster, 2000); and Michael Kranish and Marc Fisher, *Trump Revealed. An American Journey of Ambition, Ego, Money and Power.* New York: Scribner, 2016. Blair's chapter on "Born to Compete," op. cit., pp. 223ff., documents Trump's competitiveness and drive for success at an early age.

5   Marc Fisher, Will Hobson, "Donald Trump 'pretends to be his own spokesman to boast about himself.' Some reporters found the calls disturbing or even creepy; others thought they were just examples of Trump being playful." *The Independent,* May 13, 2016 at http://www.independent.co.uk/news/world/americas/us-elections/donald-trump-pretends-to-be-his-own-spokesman-to-boast-about-himself-a7027991.html (accessed August 9, 2016).

6   For my take on celebrity politics and the implosion of entertainment and politics in U.S. society, see Douglas Kellner, "Barack Obama, Media Spectacle, and Celebrity Politics" in *A Companion to Celebrity*, Edited by P. David Marshall and Sean Redmond. Malden, MA. and Oxford, UK. Wiley-Blackwell, 2015: 114–134. See also Mark Wheeler, *Celebrity Politics*. Cambridge, UK: Polity 2013. The best study of Trump, the media, and his long cultivation and exploitation of celebrity is found in Timothy L. O'Brien, *TrumpNation: The Art of Being the Donald.* New York: Grand Central Publishing, 2016 [2005].

7   Trump's book *The Art of the Deal*, co-written with Tony Schwartz (New York: Ballantine Books, 2005 [1987]), helped introduce him to a national audience and is a key source of the Trump mythology; see Blair, op. cit., 380ff. I discuss Trump's three books below.

8   Gaspin was quoted in CNN, *All Business. The Essential Donald Trump.* September 5, 2016.

9   *Quotations From Chairman Trump*, edited by Carol Pogash. New York: Rosetta Books, 2016, pp 30, 152, 153.

10 On *The Apprentice*, see Laurie Ouellette and James Hay, *Better Living Through Reality TV*. Malden, MA.: Blackwell, 2008.

11 Ravi Somaiya, "Trump's Wealth and Early Poll Numbers Complicate News Media's Coverage Decisions." *The New York Times*, July 24, 2015 at http://www.nytimes.com/2015/07/25/business/media/donald-trumps-wealth-and-poll-numbers-complicate-news-medias-coverage.html (accessed July 22, 2016).

¹² Ben Agger, *Fast Capitalism* (Champaigne-Urbana: University of Illinois Press, 1989), and *Speeding Up Fast Capitalism* (New York and London: Routledge, 2015).

¹³ Thorstein Veblen, *Theory of the Leisure Class: An Economic Study in the Evolution of Institutions*. New York: Dover, 1994 (1899).

¹⁴ Trump, *The Art of the Deal*, op. cit.

¹⁵ For the story of Trump's financial down-fall and near collapse in the 1980s and 1990s, see the detailed and well-documented narratives in Barrett, op. cit.; John O'Donnell and James Rutherford, *Trumped!: The Inside Story of the Real Donald Trump-His Cunning Rise and Spectacular Fall*. New York: Simon and Schuster, 1991; D'Antonio, op. cit; and Kranish and Fisher, op. cit.

¹⁶ Donald Trump (with Charles Leerhsen), *Trump: Surviving at the Top* (New York: Random House, 1990) and Donald Trump (with Kate Bohner), *Trump: The Art of the Comeback* (New York: Random House, 1997). Note that all of Trump's book feature his name as the title punctuated by varying subtitles that stress his business acumen and success, and all of his books have co-authors, raising the question whether Trump is really an author or a con and frontman.

¹⁷ The analysis of Fromm and Trump was first presented as "Fromm and the Counterrevolutionary Character: Frommian Reflections on Donald Trump" in a conference "The (in)sane society: Remembering Erich Fromm and the Frankfurt School," CUNY, New York, April 1, 2016. On the Frankfurt School, see the histories by Martin Jay, *The Dialectical Imagination: A History of the Frankfurt School and the Institute of Social Research, 1923–1950*. Berkeley, Cal.: University of California Press, (1973) and Rolf Wiggershaus, *The Frankfurt School: Its History, Theories, and Political Significance*. Cambridge: Mass.: The MIT Press, 1995. On the Frankfurt School social theory, see Douglas Kellner, *Critical Theory, Marxism, and Modernity*. Cambridge, UK and Baltimore, Md.: Polity Press and John Hopkins University Press, 1989.

¹⁸ On Fromm, see Daniel Burston, *The Legacy of Erich Fromm*. Cambridge, Mass: Harvard University Press, 1991; Rainer Funk, *Erich Fromm: His Life and Ideas*. Translators Ian Portman, Manuela Kunkel. New York: Continuum International Publishing Group, 2003; Lawrence J. Friedman, *The Lives of Erich Fromm: Love's Prophet*. New York: Columbia University Press, 2013.

¹⁹ Erich Fromm, *Escape from Freedom*. New York: Holt Paperbacks, 1991 (1941).

²⁰ Parenthetically, there were enough media comparisons between Trump and Hitler and fascism for Trump to say with some perhaps genuine perplexity "I'm not Hitler! I don't like the guy!" See Sam Sanders, "Trump Champions The 'Silent Majority,' But What Does That Mean In 2016?" *NPR*, January 22, 2016 at http://www.npr.org/2016/01/22/463884201/trump-champions-the-silent-majority-but-what-does-that-mean-in-2016 (accessed on July 20, 2016). At this time, Trump was asking his followers to raise their hands if they would vote for him as President, and the simultaneous raised hands going up looked like a mob of Hitler salutes! And there is a story out there that Trump keeps a book of Hitler's writings by his bedside; see O'Brien, op. cit., p. 200; the story originates from a *UPI* report, August 9, 1990, cited in O'Brien, op. cit., p. 260.

²¹ Carl Bernstein started calling Trump a neo-fascist and an American-brand fascist on CNN on June 19, 2016. See Tom Boggioni, "Carl Bernstein: Donald Trump is a 'pathological liar' and America's first 'neofascist' nominee," *Rawstory*, June 19, 2016 at http://www.rawstory.com/2016/06/carl-bernstein-donald-trump-is-a-pathological-liar-and-americas-first-neofascist-nominee/ (accessed on July 20, 2016). In an article by Adam Gopnik, "Being Honest About Trump, *The New Yorker*, July 14, 2016 at

http://www.newyorker.com/news/daily-comment/being-honest-about-trump (accessed on July 20, 2016), Gopnik comments: "It is the essence of fascism to have no single fixed form—an attenuated form of nationalism in its basic nature, it naturally takes on the colors and practices of each nation it infects. In Italy, it is bombastic and neoclassical in form; in Spain, Catholic and religious; in Germany, violent and romantic. It took forms still crazier and more feverishly sinister, if one can imagine, in Romania, whereas under Oswald Mosley, in England, its manner was predictably paternalistic and aristocratic. It is no surprise that the American face of fascism would take on the forms of celebrity television and the casino greeter's come-on, since that is as much our symbolic scene as nostalgic re-creations of Roman splendors once were Italy's." Op. cit.

22 The notion of "the magic helper" to whom the follower submits in the hopes their problems will be solved is found in Erich Fromm's *Escape from Freedom*, op. cit., pp. 174–178; on "authoritarian idolatry," see *Sane Society*, op. cit. p. 237f. *Escape from Freedom* not only critiqued Nazi ideology, the party apparatus, the concept of the Fuhrer, and the psychology of Nazi mass followers of Hitler in *Escape from Freedom*, but was also fascinated by fairy tales and magical thinking in National Socialism, a theme he expanded in later writings like *The Forgotten Language: An Introduction to the Understanding of Dreams, Fairy Tales and Myths*. New York: Random House, 1988.

23 On Trump's business failures, see Wayne Barrett, *Trump: The Greatest Show on Earth: The Deals, the Downfall, the Reinvention.* New York: Regan Books, 2016 (revision of 1992 book *Trump: The Deals and the Downfall*); O'Brien, op. cit.; D'Antonio, op. cit.; David Cay Johnston, *The Making of Donald Trump.* New York: Melville House; and Kranish and Fisher, *Trump Revealed,* op. cit. See also and "The Art of the Bad Deal. Donald Trump's Business Flops, Explained," *Newsweek,* August 8, 2018: 24–33,

24 On the centrality of the role of a Superhero in U.S. culture and politics, see Robert Jewett and John Lawrence, *The American Monomyth.* New York: Anchor, 1977 and Robert Jewett and John Lawrence, *The Myth of the American Superhero.* Grand Rapids, Mich: Wm. B. Eerdmans Publishing Company, 2002. Trump's campaign follows this model of the redemptive Hero who will slay America's enemies and return the Kingdom to peace and prosperity.

25 See the Heartfield images at https://www.google.com/search?q=John+Heartfield:+the+ meaning+of+the+Hitler+salute&biw=1600&bih=1028&tbm=isch&tbo=u&source= univ&sa=X&ved=0ahUKEwjt4KvV-N7LAhVM6WMKHUPABGMQsAQIJg (accessed March 22, 2016).

26 After bragging how his campaign was self-funded during the Republican primaries, Trump released a statement showing that much of the money he spent was paid into his own companies; see Nicholas Confessore and Sarah Cohen, "Donald Trump's Campaign, Billed as Self-Funded, Risks Little of His Fortune." *The New York Times,* February, 5, 2016 at http://www.nytimes.com/2016/02/06/us/politics/donald-trumps-campaign-billed-as-self-funded-risks-little-of-his-fortune.html?_r=0 (accessed July 29, 2016). During the Fall Presidential election, Trump is forced to court donors and raise funds, thus undercutting his claims to be the only self-financing candidate.

27 See Lauren Langman and George Lundskow, "Escape From Modernity: Authoritarianism and the Quest for the Golden Age," Paper delivered at "The Psychodynamics of Self & Society," Eighth Annual ASA Mini-Conference, Seattle, August 18, 2016.

28 Trump's vision of Latin American immigrants pouring over the border into the U.S. is a fantasy, as studies have shown that more Mexicans are returning to Mexico after working in the U.S. than coming into the country, illegal or not; see Ana Gonzalez-Barrera,

"More Mexicans Leaving Than Coming to the U.S. Net Loss of 140,000 from 2009 to 2014; Family Reunification Top Reason for Return." November 19, 2015 at http://www.pewhispanic.org/2015/11/19/more-mexicans-leaving-than-coming-to-the-u-s/ (accessed September 3, 2016).

[29] Kranish and Fisher, op. cit., pp. 27–28. It was not clear from police and media reports whether Fred Trump was marching with the Klan or was just part of the crowd that got involved in a melee with the police.

[30] Richard Hofstader, *The Paranoid Style in American Politics, and Other Essays* (New York: Knopf, 1965).

[31] On the Tea Party, see Theda Skocpol and Vanessa Williamson, *The Tea Party and the Remaking of Republican Conservatism*. New York: Oxford University Press.

[32] On the birther myth, see Michael D'Antonio, *Never Enough. Donald Trump and the Pursuit of Success*. New York: Thomas Dunne Books, 2015, pp. 283ff.

[33] Public Policy Polling reports that a "new poll finds that Trump is benefiting from a GOP electorate that thinks Barack Obama is a Muslim and was born in another country, and that immigrant children should be deported. 66% of Trump's supporters believe that Obama is a Muslim to just 12% that grant he's a Christian. 61% think Obama was not born in the United States to only 21% who accept that he was. And 63% want to amend the Constitution to eliminate birthright citizenship, to only 20% who want to keep things the way they are." *Public Policy Polling*. "Trump Supporters Think Obama is A Muslim Born in Another Country," September 01, 2015 at http://www.publicpolicypolling.com/main/2015/08/trump-supporters-think-obama-is-a-muslim-born-in-another-country.html (accessed August 3, 2016).

[34] Nicholas Confessore and Karen Yourish, "$2 Billion Worth of Free Media for Donald Trump," *The New York Times*, March 15, 2016 at http://www.nytimes.com/2016/03/16/upshot/measuring-donald-trumps-mammoth-advantage-in-free-media.html?_r=0 (accessed August 6, 2016)and Robert Schroeder, "Trump has gotten nearly $3 billion in 'free' advertising." *Marketwatch,* May 6, 2016 at http://www.marketwatch.com/story/trump-has-gotten-nearly-3-billion-in-free-advertising-2016-05-06 (accessed August 6, 2016).

[35] On Trump's business failures, see Note 15 above.

[36] At the Republican convention, Trump insisted that "you won't hear any lies here," For documentation of Trump's Big and little lies, see Hank Berrien, "Lyin' Donald: 101 Of Trump's Greatest Lies," *Dailywire*, April 11, 2016 at http://www.dailywire.com/news/4834/trumps-101-lies-hank-berrien (accessed August 8, 2016).

[37] On Trump's appeal to gun owners, see Daniel Hayes, "Donald Trump Takes Aim," *The New York Times*, August 20, 2016 at http://www.nytimes.com/2016/08/21/opinion/campaign-stops/donald-trump-takes-aim.html?_r=0 (accessed August 24, 2016).

[38] In an article subtitled "How the Christian right came to support a thrice-married adulterer," see Daniel K. Williams "Why Values Voters Value Donald Trump," *The New York Times*, August 20, 2016 at http://www.nytimes.com/2016/08/21/opinion/sunday/why-values-voters-value-donald-trump.html (accessed August 24, 2016).

[39] Evan Osmos "The Fearful and the Frustrated: Donald Trump's nationalist coalition takes shape – for now" *The New Yorker*, August 31, 2015 at http://www.newyorker.com/magazine/2015/08/31/the-fearful-and-the-frustrated (accessed July 22, 2016).

[40] Osmos, op. cit.

[41] On Fromm and "authoritarian idolatry," see *Sane Society*, op. cit. p. 237f.

[42] See Jackson Katz, *Man Enough? Donald Trump, Hillary C, and the Politics of Presidential Masculinity*. Northampton, Mass.: Interlink Publishing Company, 2016.

[43] See the video at CNN, http://www.cnn.com/videos/tv/2015/11/26/donald-trump-mocks-reporter-with-disability-berman-sot-ac.cnn (accessed August 9, 2016).

[44] In a classic example of Freudian projection, over the weekend of August 6–7, Trump accused Hillary Clinton of being unbalanced, coming unhinged, and being mentally unstable, previously the charges being deployed against Trump which I discuss below using Fromm's categories. See Jose A. DelReal, "Trump, in series of scathing personal attacks, questions Clinton's mental health," *Washington Post*, Aug. 7, 2016 at https://www.washingtonpost.com/news/post-politics/wp/2016/08/06/trump-in-series-of-scathing-personal-attacks-questions-clintons-mental-health/ (accessed August 10, 2016). In a speech in West Bend, Wisconsin, on August 16, 2016, Trump called Clinton a "bigot," a charge frequently tossed at him.

[45] Maggie Haberman, "Donald Trump Retweets Post With Quote From Mussolini," *The New York Times*, February 28, 2106 at http://www.nytimes.com/politics/first-draft/2016/02/28/donald-trump-retweets-post-likening-him-to-mussolini/ (accessed August 8, 2016).

[46] Media Matters Staff, "Ted Koppel Compares Donald Trump To Benito Mussolini. Koppel: Trump And Mussolini Both 'Say Very Little In Terms Of Substance, But The Manner In Which They Say It Gets The Crowds Excited,'" *Media Matters,* December 16, 2015 at http://mediamatters.org/video/2015/12/16/ted-koppel-compares-donald-trump-to-benito-muss/207564 (accessed August 9, 2016).

[47] For my take on celebrity politics and the implosion of entertainment and politics in U.S. society, see Douglas Kellner, "Barack Obama, Media Spectacle, and Celebrity Politics" in *A Companion to Celebrity*, Edited by P. David Marshall and Sean Redmond. Malden, MA. and Oxford, UK. Wiley-Blackwell, 2015: 114–134. See also Mark Wheeler, *Celebrity Politics*. Cambridge, UK: Polity 2013.

[48] Erich Fromm, *The Anatomy of Human Destructiveness*. New York: Holt, Rinehart, and Winston, 1973.

[49] See Sigmund Freud, *The Ego and the Id* (The Standard Edition of the Complete Psychological Works of Sigmund Freud). New York: W. W. Norton & Company, 1990 [1923]. For Freud, the Id represents the irrational and aggressive components of the personality, while the Ego represents the rational self which can suffer, however, narcissistic tendencies that undercut its rationality. We shall see below how Fromm builds on Freud's psychoanalytic categories in ways that they can be applied to demagogues like Hitler and Trump and mass movements of authoritarian populism, or neo-fascism.

[50] See D'Antonio, op. cit. and Blair, op. cit.

[51] On the Frankfurt School theory of the authoritarian personality, see the books cited in Note 17. See also T.W. Adorno, et al *The Authoritarian Personality*. New York: Norton Books, 1969.

[52] Erich Fromm, *The Anatomy of Human Destructiveness*. New York: Holt, Reinhart and Winston, 1973, p. 282.

[53] See Erich Fromm, *The Sane Society*. New York: Holt, Reinhart and Winston, 1955, and, *The Anatomy of Human Destructiveness*. New York: Holt, Rinehart, and Winston, 1973.

[54] Fromm, *Sane Society,* op. cit. p. 36.

[55] Fromm, *The Anatomy of Human Destructiveness*, op. cit. pp. 406–407.

[56] D'Antonio, op. cit. California Congresswoman Karen Bass (D-Cal) began a petition to request that mental health professionals evaluate Trump for Narcissistic Personality

Disorder (NPD), insisting that he had all the symptoms. See Wayne Rojas, "Karen Bass Wants Mental Health Professionals to Evaluate Trump. Calif. Democrat suspects GOP nominee has Narcissistic Personality Disorder," *Rollcall,* Aug 3, 2016 at http://www.rollcall.com/news/politics/karen-bass-wants-mental-health-professionals-to-evaluate-trump#sthash.75ABMmmT.dpuf (accessed August 2, 2016). On the traits of Narcissistic Personality Disorder and how Trump embodies them, see Bill Blum, "The Psychopathology of Donald Trump," *Truthdig.* July 31, 2016 at http://www.truthdig.com/report/item/the_psychopathology_of_donald_trump_20160731/ (accessed August 2, 2016).

57 Barrett, op. cit. pp. 342ff.

58 See Barrett, op. cit.; D'Antonio, op. cit.; Johnston, op. cit. and John O'Donnell and James Rutherford, *Trumped!: The Inside Story of the Real Donald Trump-His Cunning Rise and Spectacular Fall.* New York: Simon and Schuster, 1991.

59 On Fromm's concept of character orientations, see *The Sane Society*, op. cit. and *Man for Himself: An Inquiry Into the Psychology of Ethics.* New York: Holt, 1990.

60 See Barrett, op. cit., p. 330.

61 Thorstein Veblen, op. cit.

62 On rational choice theory that argues that voters pursue what they see as their economic interests, see the entry on "Rational Choice Theory," in *Encyclopædia Britannica* at https://www.britannica.com/topic/rational-choice-theory (accessed August 6, 2016).

63 Henry A. Giroux, "Donald Trump and the Plague of Atomization in a Neoliberal Age," *Truthout*, August 8, 2016 http://www.truth-out.org/opinion/item/37133-donald-trump-and-the-plague-of-atomization-in-a-neoliberal-age (accessed August 9, 2016).

64 Donald J. Trump 6:08 AM – 6 Nov 2015 at https://twitter.com/realDonaldTrump (accessed March 22, 2016).

65 Gabriel Arana, "Here Are All The Ugly Remarks Trump Has Made About Megyn Kelly. As if to prove her point, the reality TV star has continued to spew sexist vitriol after the presidential debate." *The Huffington Post*, August 8, 2015 at http://www.huffingtonpost.com/entry/trump-megyn-kelly-debate-fox-news_us_55c5f6b3e4b0f73b20b989a7 (accessed August 10, 2016).

66 Bill Trott and Steve Holland, "Donald Trump Drawing Fire From All Corners Of GOP," The Huffington Post, August 8, 2015 at http://www.huffingtonpost.com/entry/donald-trump-drawing-fire-from-all-corners-of-gop_us_55c668dde4b0f73b20b9937e (accessed August 10, 2016).

67 The *Fox News* statement can be found at http://www.mediaite.com/online/read-the-statement-from-fox-news-about-trumps-extreme-six-obsession-with-megyn-kelly/ (accessed March 22, 2016).

68 Josh Voorhees, Donald Trump Is Trying to Undermine the Democratic Process Itself," *Slate,* August 2, 2016 at http://www.slate.com/blogs/the_slatest/2016/08/02/trump_s_rigged_comments_are_the_most_dangerous_thing_he_s_said_yet.html (accessed August 5, 2016).

69 Maureen Dowd, "Donald Trump's Disturbia," *New York Times,* July 23, 2016 at http://www.nytimes.com/2016/07/24/opinion/sunday/donald-trumps-disturbia.html?_r=0 (accessed July 25, 2016).

70 On Trumps' threat to form "Anti-certain candidate PACs" to defeat those Republicans who opposed him, see Phillip Rucker's interview with Trump appended to Chris Cilizza, "Donald Trump's *Washington Post* interview should make Republicans panic," *Washington Post,* August 3, 2016 at https://www.washingtonpost.com/news/the-fix/wp/2016/08/03/donald-trump-has-a-secret-state-strategy-that-you-cant-know-about/ (accessed August 4, 2016).

71 Fromm, *The Anatomy of Human Destructiveness,* op. cit. pp. 325ff.

72 Fromm, op. cit. pp. 350ff.

73 For an account of both Trump's marriage and financial disasters, see Blair, op. cit., 385–452.

74 Sam Sanders, "Trump Champions The 'Silent Majority,' But What Does That Mean In 2016?" *NPR,* January 22, 2016 at http://www.npr.org/2016/01/22/463884201/trump-champions-the-silent-majority-but-what-does-that-mean-in-2016 (accessed August 22, 2016).

75 Philip Roth's novel *The Plot Against America* (Boston New York: Houghton Mifflin Company, 2004) provides an alternate view of history in which Lindbergh is elected President and proceeds to implant fascism in America, with a character uncannily like Donald Trump. Sinclair Lewis' 1935 novel *It Can't Happen Here* (New York: New American Library, 1970) also has a Trump-like demagogue elected to the presidency who implants an American fascism agenda.

76 Libby Nelson, "'America First': Donald Trump's slogan has a deeply bigoted backstory," July 22, 2016 at http://www.vox.com/2016/7/20/12198760/america-first-donald-trump-convention (accessed July 22, 2016).

77 Here is a video that compares Melania Trump's speech with the lifted paragraphs from Michelle Obama = https://www.washingtonpost.com/news/monkey-cage/wp/2016/07/20/melania-trump-and-the-culture-of-cheating-in-eastern-european-schools/ (accessed August 28, 2016), and a YouTube = https://www.youtube.com/watch?v=RcbiGsDMmCM (accessed August 28, 2016). And here is the transcript of the passages in question = http://www.cnn.com/TRANSCRIPTS/1607/19/es.01.html (accessed August 2, 2016).

78 Brett Neely, "Trump Speechwriter Accepts Responsibility For Using Michelle Obama's Words," *National Public Radio,* July 20, 2016 at http://www.npr.org/2016/07/20/486758596/trump-speechwriter-accepts-responsibility-for-using-michelle-obamas-words (accessed August 8, 2016).

79 "Bushspeak and the Politics of Lying, op. cit.

80 Harry G. Frankfurt, *On Bullshit.* Princeton University Press, 2005. Several commentators noted the relevance of Frankfurt's concept of bullshit to Trump's discursive habits. See Jeet Heer, "Donald Trump Is Not a Liar. He's something worse: a bullshit artist." December 1, 2015 at https://newrepublic.com/article/124803/donald-trump-not-liar (accessed August 28, 2016), and Karoli Kuns, "Fareed Zakaria Explains In Detail Why He Considers Trump A 'Bullshit Artist.'" *Crooks and Liars,* August 8, 2016 at http://crooksandliars.com/2016/08/fareed-zakaria-explains-detail-while-he (accessed August 28, 2016).

81 For a *Politifact* documentation of Trump's lies, see Aaron Sharockman, "The truth (so far) behind the 2016 campaign," June 29th, 2016 *at* http://www.politifact.com/truth-o-meter/article/2016/jun/29/fact-checking-2016-clinton-trump/ (accessed August 28, 2016).

82 Brett Neely, "Trump Speechwriter Accepts Responsibility For Using Michelle Obama's Words," *National Public Radio,* July 20, 2016 at http://www.npr.org/2016/07/20/486758596/trump-speechwriter-accepts-responsibility-for-using-michelle-obamas-words (accessed July 28, 2016).

83 Adele M. Stan, "Republican National Convention Follows Witch-Burning Script," The men behind Trump understand the historical impulse to quash female power. *AlterNet,* July 19, 2016 at http://www.alternet.org/right-wing/republican-national-convention-follows-witch-burning-script (accessed July 28, 2016).

84 Statement by FBI Director James B. Comey on the Investigation of Secretary Hillary Clinton's Use of a Personal E-Mail System at https://www.fbi.gov/news/pressrel/press-releases/statement-by-fbi-director-james-b-comey-on-the-investigation-of-secretary-hillary-clinton2019s-use-of-a-personal-e-mail-system (accessed July 28, 2016).

85 Brendan Dorsey, "Donald Trump's Veterans Advisor Says Hillary Clinton Should Be 'Shot For Treason" *Time*, July 20, 2016 at http://time.com/4415120/donald-trump-hillary-clinton-shot/ (accessed July 28, 2016).

86 Glenn Kessler and Michelle Ye Hee Lee, "Fact-checking Donald Trump's acceptance speech at the 2016 RNC," *Washington Post*, July 22, 2016 at https://www.washingtonpost.com/news/fact-checker/wp/2016/07/22/fact-checking-donald-trumps-acceptance-speech-at-the-2016-rnc/ (accessed July 28, 2016).

87 Jennifer Rubin, "Final grade for the Republican National Convention: 'D" *Washington Post*, July 22, 2016 at https://www.washingtonpost.com/blogs/right-turn/wp/2016/07/22/final-grade-for-the-republican-national-convention-d/?utm_term=.523600a2c91a (accessed July 28, 2016).

88 Frank Bruni, "The Republicans' Big Hot Mess," *New York Times*, June 18, 2016 at http://www.nytimes.com/2016/06/19/opinion/sunday/the-republicans-big-hot-mess.html?_r=0 (accessed July 20, 2016) and POLITICO Magazine, The Worst Convention in U.S. History? We asked historians to tell us how the 2016 Republican National Convention stacks up." POLITICO, July 22, 2016 at http://www.politico.com/magazine/story/2016/07/rnc-2016-worst-convention-historians-214091 (accessed July 24, 2016).

89 The intervention did not take place, but Trump did endorse Ryan and McCain reading his tepid endorsement from note cards and not looking directly up into the camera, signaling that he lacked enthusiasm and was making the endorsements under duress.

90 Nick Corasaniti and Maggie Haberman, "Donald Trump Suggests 'Second Amendment People' Could Act Against Hillary Clinton," *The New York Times*, August. 9, 2016 *at* http://www.nytimes.com/2016/08/10/us/politics/donald-trump-hillary-clinton.html?_r=0 (accessed August 11, 2016).

91 Janet Allon, "10 Political and Psychological Observers Who Think Trump May Have Gone Off the Deep End," *AlterNet*, August 1, 2016 at http://www.alternet.org/election-2016/trump-clinically-crazy-increasing-number-psychologists-and-commentators-think-so (accessed July 22, 2016). Psychiatrist Matthew Golding wrote that while psychiatrists were not supposed to speculate on the mental health of someone who they had not had professional sessions with, "You don't have to be a psychiatrist to know that there's something seriously wrong with Trump and that he is unfit for the presidency." See "No diagnosis needed for Trump," *Los Angeles Times*, August 23, 2016: A11.Recent unhinged rants have raised questions about the candidate's mental state.

92 Dan Roberts and Haroon Siddique, "Donald Trump appoints Breitbart chief Stephen Bannon to lead campaign," *The Guardian*, August 17, 2016 at https://www.theguardian.com/us-news/2016/aug/17/donald-trump-stephen-bannon-breitbart-news-kellyanne-conway (accessed August 17, 2016). The most detailed background story on Bannon and the Breibart operation is found at Joshua Green, "This Man Is the Most Dangerous Political Operative in America. Steve Bannon runs the new vast right-wing conspiracy—and he wants to take down both Hillary Clinton and Jeb Bush." *Bloomberg.com*, October 8, 2015 at http://www.bloomberg.com/politics/graphics/2015-steve-bannon/ (accessed August 11, 2016).

93 Aaron Blake, "Donald Trump's hire of Breitbart News chief is a middle finger to the GOP establishment," *The Washington Post*, August 17, 2016 at https://www.washingtonpost.com/news/the-fix/wp/2016/08/17/donald-trumps-hire-of-the-breitbart-news-chief-is-a-middle-finger-to-the-gop-establishment/ (accessed August 17, 2016).

94 Michael Moore, by contrast, thinks that Trump is deliberately sabotaging his campaign because he really doesn't want to be President. See *"*Michael Moore: Trump Is Self Sabotaging His Campaign Because He Never Really Wanted the Job in the First Place,"He's running for president to get a better deal for "The Apprentice." *Huffingtonpost*, August 16, 2016 at http://www.huffingtonpost.com/michael-moore/trump-self-sabotage_b_11545026.html (accessed August 17, 2016). Others speculated that Trump, perhaps in league with Roger Ailes and Steven Bannon, was really planning to create a new media empire; see Neal Gabler, "To Trump, Even Losing Is Victory," *New York Times*, August 20, 2016: A17.

95 This analysis was offered by Rachel Maddow on *The Rachel Maddow Show* on August 23, 2016.

96 See Lauren Gambino, "Trump's 'deeply un-American' stance on immigration prompts legal concerns. Experts warn Republican nominee's plan to restrict immigration on the basis of ideology is impractical and could be unconstitutional Trump says no immigration to US without 'extreme vetting,'" *The Guardian*, August 17, 2016 at https://www.theguardian.com/us-news/2016/aug/17/trump-immigration-plan-us-constitution (accessed August 17, 2016).

97 Hadas Gold, "Donald Trump: We're going to 'open up' libel laws," *Politico*, February 26, 2016 at http://www.politico.com/blogs/on-media/2016/02/donald-trump-libel-laws-219866#ixzz4JOVPzBwQ (accessed August 27, 2016).

98 See the Trump biographies that document his history of racial bigotry and discrimination in Note 4, especially Kranish and Fisher, op. cit, pp. 53–57.

99 Maria La Ganga, "Clinton slams Trump's 'racist ideology' that ushers hate groups into mainstream. Positioning herself as the representative of a tolerant and open-minded US, she derided her rival as a darling of the 'alt-right' and a soulmate of David Duke," *The Guardian*, August 25, 2016 at https://www.theguardian.com/us-news/2016/aug/25/hillary-clinton-alt-right-racism-speech-donald-trump-nevada (accessed August 27, 2016). The same day, the Clinton campaign released a video on television that presented a broad array of the "alt-right" spokespeople from fringe white suprematicists to David Duke, a former grand wizard of the Ku Klux Klan, all supporting Trump for President.

100 Jon Swaine, Lauren Gambino, and Richard Luscombe, "Trump campaign chief Steve Bannon is registered voter at vacant Florida home. Exclusive: Bannon's enrollment is apparent violation of crucial swing state's election law requiring voters to be legal residents of county they register in," *The Guardian*, August 26, 2016 at https://www.theguardian.com/us-news/2016/aug/26/steve-bannon-florida-registered-vote-donald-trump (accessed August 27, 2016) and Tom McCarthy, "Steve Bannon, Trump campaign CEO, faced domestic violence charges." *The Guardian*, August 26, 2016 at https://www.theguardian.com/us-news/2016/aug/26/steve-bannon-domestic-violence-trump-campaign-ceo (accessed August 26, 2016). Soon after, it was revealed that Bannon's ex-wife said in divorce papers that "her ex-husband had objected to sending their twin daughters to an elite Los Angeles academy because he "didn't want the girls going to school with Jews". See *Associated Press*, "Trump campaign CEO Stephen Bannon denies antisemitic remarks," *The Guardian*, August 27, 2016 at https://www.theguardian.com/us-news/2016/aug/27/trump-campaign-ceo-stephen-bannon-denies-antisemitic-remarks (accessed August 27, 2016).

[101] Dan Roberts, "Trump's slump in Nascar country deepens Republican fears of defeat. Even at the Hall of Fame in North Carolina, pessimism is rising as fast as the billionaire falls in the polls, threatening GOP control of Congress," 29 August 2016.

[102] Karen Yourish and Larry Buchanan, "At Least 110 Republican Leaders Won't Vote for Donald Trump. Here's When They Reached Their Breaking Point. This list includes current and former members of Congress, governors and high-level officials from Republican administrations. People shaded in blue have said they will vote for Hillary Clinton." *New York Times*, August 29, 2016 at http://www.nytimes.com/interactive/2016/08/29/us/politics/at-least-110-republican-leaders-wont-vote-for-donald-trump-heres-when-they-reached-their-breaking-point.html?hp&action=click&pgtype=Homepage&clickSource=story-heading&module=b-lede-package-region&region=top-news&WT.nav=top-news&_r=0 (accessed August 28, 2016).

[103] Eli Stokols, "Trump might already be out of time. With negative perceptions hardened, his late adjustments on policy and rhetoric could sway too few people to matter." *Politico*, August 28, 2016 at http://www.com/story/2016/08/trump-campaign-turn-around-out-of-time-227457 (accessed August 28, 2016).

[104] Nick Gass, "A psychiatrist needs to examine Trump," *Politico*, August 29, 2016 at http://www.politico.com/story/2016/08/trump-mental-health-mika-brzezinski-227492 (accessed August 28, 2016).

[105] Tom McCarthy, "Mike Pence praises 'plainspoken' Trump amid furor over Dwyane Wade remarks." *The Guardian*, August 28, 2016 at https://www.theguardian.com/us-news/2016/aug/28/mike-pence-donald-trump-dwyane-wade-comments (accessed August 28, 2016).

[106] Alan Rappeport, "'He Used Us as Props': Conservative Hispanics Deplore Donald Trump's Speech," *The New York Times*, September 1, 2016 at http://www.nytimes.com/2016/09/02/us/politics/gop-hispanic-reaction-trump.html?_r=0 (accessed August 29, 2016).

[107] Amita Kelly, "Trump Surrogate Tweets Cartoon Of Hillary Clinton In Blackface," *NPR*, August 29, 2016 at http://www.npr.org/2016/08/29/491858156/trump-surrogate-tweets-cartoon-of-hillary-clinton-in-blackface (accessed August 29, 2016).

[108] Elisha Fieldstadt and Ali Vitali, "Donald Trump's 'Star of David' Tweet About Hillary Clinton Posted Weeks Earlier on Racist Feed," *NBC News*, July 4, 2016 at http://www.nbcnews.com/politics/2016-election/donald-trump-s-star-david-tweet-about-hillary-clinton-posted-n603161 (accessed August 29, 2016).

[109] Lyamiche Alcindor, "Leaked Script Shows What Advisers Want Donald Trump to Say at Black Church," *The New York Times*, September 1, 2016 at http://www.nytimes.com/2016/09/02/us/politics/donald-trump-black-voters-wayne-jackson.html?_r=0 (accessed September 2, 2016).

[110] Victor Fiorillo, "Rev. Herb Lusk says he wasn't invited to Trump's meeting with African-American leaders, which is being held Friday at his church's banquet hall," *Phillymag*, September 1, 2016 at http://cdn.phillymag.com/wp-content/uploads/2016/09/donald-trump-philly-visit-herb-lusk-church.jpg (accessed September 2, 2016).

[111] Ruth Marcus, "Trump just hired the Captain Ahab of Clinton haters," *Washington Post*, September 2, 2016 at https://www.washingtonpost.com/opinions/trump-just-hired-the-captain-ahab-of-clinton-haters/2016/09/02/2b5f45b0-713f-11e6-8365-19e428a975e_story.html?tid=pm_opinions_pop_b&utm_term=.028b5eb144af (accessed September 2, 2016).

[112] Aaron Blake, "Welcome to the next, most negative presidential election of our lives," *Washington Post*, July 29, 2016 at https://www.washingtonpost.com/news/the-fix/wp/2016/07/29/clinton-and-trump-accept-their-nominations-by-telling-you-what-you-should-vote-against/ (accessed September 2, 2016).

[113] Steve Eder and Meagan Twohey, "Donald Trump's Donation Is His Latest Brush With Campaign Fund Rules," *The New York Times*, September 6, 2016 at http://www.nytimes.com/2016/09/07/us/politics/donald-trump-pam-bondi.html?_r=0 (accessed September 8, 2016).

[114] Lauer was criticized for throwing tough questions at Clinton and then repeatedly interrupting her, while failing to do so with Trump; see Michael M. Grynbau, "Matt Lauer Fields Storm of Criticism Over Clinton-Trump Forum," *New York Times*, September 8, 2016 at http://www.nytimes.com/2016/09/08/us/politics/matt-lauer-forum.html (accessed September 8, 2016).

[115] Nicole Gaouette, "Former intel briefer: 'Wildly unlikely' Trump account correct," *CNN Politics*, September 9, 2016 at http://www.cnn.com/2016/09/08/politics/donald-trump-intelligence-briefing-clinton-obama/index.html (accessed September 9, 2016).

[116] "Trump interview broadcast on Russian propaganda outlet – campaign live," *The Guardian*, September 9, 2016 at https://www.theguardian.com/us-news/live/2016/sep/09/donald-trump-russia-tv-campaign-hillary-clinton (accessed September 9, 2016).

[117] Trump's interview and the Russian connections of Trump and his campaign are dissected in Jose A. DelReal, "Trump attacks U.S. foreign policy, political press corps on state-owned Russian television network," *The Washington Post*," September 8, 2016, at https://www.washingtonpost.com/news/post-politics/wp/2016/09/08/trump-attacks-u-s-foreign-policy-political-press-corps-in-state-owned-russian-television-network/?tid=pm_politics_pop_b (accessed September 9, 2016).

[118] Mary Louise, "Kelly Foreign Policy Experts Push Back On Trump's Iranian Ships," *NPR*, September 13, 2016 at http://www.npr.org/2016/09/13/493721843/foreign-policy-experts-push-back-on-trumps-remark-to-shoot-iranian-ships-out-of (accessed September 15, 2016).

[119] The same day, statistics were released that indicated incomes were up and poverty rates were down in the Census Bureau's annual report that showed the most significant improvement in both indicators in decades, providing good economic news for the Obama administration and Clinton's campaign. See Don Lee, "Incomes up, poverty rate down in new census data," *Los Angeles Times*, September 14, 2016: A1.

[120] Aaron Blake, "Here are the juiciest Colin Powell comments about Trump and Clinton from his hacked emails," *The Washington Post*, September 14, 2016 at https://www.washingtonpost.com/news/the-fix/wp/2016/09/14/here-are-the-juiciest-colin-powell-comments-about-trump-and-clinton-from-his-leaked-emails/ (accessed September 15, 2016).

[121] Sarah K. Burris, "Ky Gov. Matt Bevin predicts 'shedding of the blood of tyrants and patriots' if Clinton is elected," *Raw Story*, September 12, 2016 at http://www.rawstory.com/2016/09/ky-gov-matt-bevin-predicts-shedding-of-the-blood-of-tyrants-and-patriots-if-clinton-is-elected/ (accessed September 15, 2016).

[122] Kurt Eichenwald, "How the Trump organization's foreign business ties could upend U.S. national security." *Newsweek*, September 14, 2016 at http://www.newsweek.com/2016/09/23/donald-trump-foreign-business-deals-national-security-498081.html (accessed September 15, 2016).

[123] Alan Rappeport, "Donald Trump, Interrupted. He Calls Flint Pastor Who Cut In 'a Nervous Mess.' *The New York Times*, September 15, 2016 at http://www.nytimes.com/2016/09/16/us/politics/donald-trump-flint-pastor.html (accessed September 15, 2016).

[124] Robert Costa, "Trump releases letter from his doctor, saying he takes cholesterol-lowering drug, is overweight," *The Washington Post*, September 15, 2016, at 11:20 at

https://www.washingtonpost.com/news/post-politics/wp/2016/09/15/trump-shares-letter-from-his-doctor-saying-he-takes-cholesterol-lowering-drug-is-overweight/ (accessed September 15, 2016).

[125] Pema Levy, "Ivanka Trump Shuts Down in the Face of Basic Questions From *Cosmopolitan* Magazine. 'I think that you have a lot of negativity in these questions.'" *Mother Jones*, September 15, 2016 at http://www.motherjones.com/politics/2016/09/ivanka-trump-shuts-down-faced-basic-questions-cosmopolitan-magazine (accessed September 15, 2016).

[126] Robert Costa, "Trump won't say Obama was born in United States, feels bullish as poll numbers rise." *The Washington Post*, September 15, 2016, at https://www.washingtonpost.com/politics/trump-defiant-as-polls-rise-wont-say-obama-was-born-in-united-states/2016/09/15/48913162-7b61-11e6-ac8e-cf8e0dd91dc7_story.html?hpid=hp_hp-top-table-main_trump-745pm%3Ahomepage%2Fstory&tid=a_inl (accessed September 16, 2016).

[127] For the *Guardian* collection of tweets and media comments on the unfolding of the Trump (pseudo)birther spectacle, see "Trump finally admits Obama was born in the US – campaign live," *The* Guardian, September 16, 2016 at https://www.theguardian.com/us-news/live/2016/sep/16/donald-trump-barack-obama-birther-movement-election-live (accessed September 16, 2016).

[128] Jenna Johnson, "Trump admits Obama was born in U.S., but falsely blames Clinton for starting rumors," *The Washington Post*, September 16, 2016, at https://www.washingtonpost.com/news/post-politics/wp/2016/09/16/trump-admits-obama-was-born-in-u-s-but-falsely-blames-clinton-for-starting-rumors/?hpid=hp_hp-top-table-main_trump-1145am%3Ahomepage%2Fstory (accessed September 15, 2016).

[129] See Michael Barbaro, "Donald Trump Clung to 'Birther' Lie for Years, and Still Isn't Apologetic," *The New York Times*, September 16, 2016 at http://www.nytimes.com/2016/09/17/us/politics/donald-trump-obama-birther.html?ribbon-ad-idx=4&rref=politics&module=Ribbon&version=context&region=Header&action=click&contentCollection=Politics&pgtype=article&_r=1 (accessed September 17, 2016).

[130] Richard Luscombe, "Trump hints at Clinton's assassination again after retracting 'birther' theory." *The Guardian*, September 16, 2016 at https://www.theguardian.com/us-news/2016/sep/16/trump-miami-clinton-disarm-security-obama-birther (accessed September 16, 2016).

[131] Chris Cillizza, "Don't look now: Donald Trump has all the momentum in the 2016 race," *The Washington Post*, September 14, 2016, at https://www.washingtonpost.com/news/the-fix/wp/2016/09/14/dont-look-now-donald-trump-has-all-the-momentum-in-the-2016-race/?hpid=hp_hp-top-table-main_fixpoll-835a%3Ahomepage%2Fstory (accessed September 15, 2016). By September 16, 2016 Trump was beginning to brag again on television that he was now ahead in the polls.

[132] For a full account, see http://wpo.st/Aq542)

[133] Herbert Marcuse, *One-Dimensional Man*. Boston: Beacon Press, 1964.

[134] Donald J. Trump cited in Kranisch and Fisher, op. cit., p. 94.

ABOUT THE AUTHOR

Douglas Kellner is George Kneller Chair in the Philosophy of Education at UCLA and is author of many books on social theory, politics, history, and culture, including *Herbert Marcuse and the Crisis of Marxism, Camera Politica; Critical Theory, Marxism, and Modernity; Jean Baudrillard: From Marxism to Postmodernism and Beyond*; works in social theory and cultural studies such as *Media Culture*; a trilogy of books on postmodern theory with Steve Best; a trilogy of books on the media and the Bush administration; and *Media Spectacle and Insurrection, 2011: From the Arab Uprisings to Occupy Everywhere* His website is at https://pages.gseis.ucla.edu/faculty/kellner/

Printed in the United States
by Baker & Taylor Publisher Services